Nectar of Nondual Truth

CONTENTS

10 Hearing Vedanta
by SRV Staff
Words are essentially important. Understanding them in proper context is equally important. So let us not "get lost in translation"......

12 Knowing After
by Babaji Bob Kindler
The fact that people come to know anything at all is based upon the fact that their ignorance gets dispelled in the learning process. Philosophically speaking, this is a key facet of human growth, which explains the all-abiding Wisdom that we see in the seers and luminaries, and reveals the illusory nature of ignorance.

16 When Consciousness is in Charge
by Brother Tadrupa
Nondual Awareness returns to its original Throne when the usurper called *ahamkara*, the ego, is relegated back in its proper place — as a ripe and ready servant to man's well-informed intellectual propensities.

18 Ahimsa: The Virtue of Nonviolence
by Swami Brahmeshananda
It has always been a standing axiom of existence that the nature of reality is nonviolent, its essence ever-peaceful. When human beings come to adhere to this fact, they transform harmful acts into beneficial ones, and erratic human nature into Divinity Itself.

25 Qi: Health & Immortality in Daoism
by Lam Fuho
Though the word Qi in Taoism has undergone many misinterpretations over the centuries, and suffered many inadequate definitions, it nevertheless has withstood the test of time to stand forth as one of the world's most valuable examples of healing balance.

34 Great is Peace
by Rabbi Rami Shapiro
Among the world's oldest major religious traditions, Judaism is replete with teachings that both exemplify and promote peace and nonviolence. In the Psalms it is stated that "only Peace is unconditional." Beings must realize this and hold it sacrosanct, above all.

36 The Mystical Power of Islam
by Sheikh Nur Al-Jerrahi
Islam, the world's youngest religion, and despite common misunderstanding, is also among the world's most peacefully-inclined religions as well, as this deep and engaging article by Lex Hixon, SRV's founder, reveals.

39 The Reality of Peace
by Swami Sunirmalananda
Despite the presence of so many warlike beings on the planet, and a multitude of warring factions, the quest for Peace still occupies the hearts and minds of the Truth-loving minority here — as instanced by the simple yet profound reasoning found in this article.

43 Advaita Vedanta & Guru-bhakti
by Swami Aseshananda
How can two apparently contrasting principles occupy the attention of the freedom-aspiring mind? The better question might be "How can these two exist without one another?" This article reveals how Nonduality and deep faith in the Guru Principle perfectly coexist.

46 Spiritual Tools for Peace of Mind
by Annapurna Sarada
For the elimination of stress and the attainment of peace of mind, the practitioner must turn to the Witness, must become the Seer, leaving off identification with the unripe ego that identifies mistakenly with the psycho/physical being and its collection of insentient coverings, called *upadhis*.

"So then, let us escape for a few hours into the radiant and inwardly redolent realm of the Wisdom Mother, and just lay, unreservedly, in Her womb of contemplative Peace; there we can relish the Truth, uninterruptedly...."

Publisher's Page

Sarada Ramakrishna Vivekananda – SRV Associations
"Setting the feet of humanity on the path of Universal Truth."

Notes on an Advaitic Journal

At the basis of Advaita as the philosophy of Shankara and his gurus, there is Advaita as experience. Advaita as experience represents that supreme place where all diversity merges in its Essence. It is not combatant or immiscible with qualified or dualistic approaches, but rather provides them their place of consummate arrival. Where actual practice rather than mere book learning is emphasized, where religion, philosophy and spirituality are not separate from one another, where knowledge and love, reason and devotion, are never divorced from each other, there does the truth of authentic nonduality effloresce.

Historically speaking, experiential Advaita originated with the ancient Rishis. Therefore, the Upanisads contain the nondual truths of the Vedas which declare: idam mahabhutam anantam aparam vijnanaghana eva, *"This great Being is endless and without limit. It is a mass of indivisible Consciousness only."*

SRV Associations & Universality

The SRV Associations are part of a worldwide movement of spiritual aspirants devoted to the study and practice of Vedanta and Divine Mother Wisdom. The ideals of this ancient pathway to God, exemplified in the lives of Sri Sarada Devi, Sri Ramakrishna and Swami Vivekananda, are the original and eternal perfection of the Soul and its inherent oneness with Reality, the manifesting of divinity in our lives, selfless service of all beings as God, and reverence for the ultimate unity of all sacred traditions. To this end our purpose is to study, worship, and contemplate Truth so that spirituality may flourish. This is the Advaitic way — *"None else but Self, none other than Mother."*

Nectar's Mission — Advaita-Satya-Amritam

In Sanskrit, *amrita*, nectar also means Immortality – and this is, indeed, what we are offering: opportunities to become aware of this Amrita that is our very Essence via the rarefied teachings from Vedanta and the World Religions and Philosophies that appear in each issue of Nectar.

Nectar of Non-Dual Truth is SRV Associations' heartfelt offering of highest Wisdom to the human community. It is the sincerest form of love and service we know to disseminate nondual Truth and teachings which transmit pure knowledge, pure love, and true universality. Through Nectar we are working out SRV's mission of spiritual upliftment and education. Please join us; this is a universal movement.

Keeping Nectar in Print

Nectar is a free magazine that can be ordered in printed form online at www.srv.org, and it can also be viewed online. (play.google.com/books) However, substantial donations are needed every year to maintain this publication in print. Why is this important?

1 – Printed Nectars are best for person to person and organization to organization dissemination of these ennobling teachings that deepen one's own spiritual life and engender knowledge of, acceptance, and reverence for all other paths.

2 – Only printed copies can reach those who do not have access to online viewing, including prison inmates, who are a particular focus of SRV's social seva.

Use the subscription/donation form provided at the back of this issue to send a check or credit card payment to SRV Associations, P.O. Box 1364, Honokaa, HI., 96727, or donate online at www.srv.org. Your donations are tax deductible.

With reverent gratitude, we heartily thank the contributing writers of this issue of Nectar of Nondual Truth, who have so graciously and selflessly shared the wisdom of their respective traditions and practices.

Staff of Nectar of Nondual Truth

Publisher
Sarada Ramakrishna Vivekananda Associations
an Annual Publication
For more information concerning the SRV Associations or Nectar of Nondual Truth please contact:
SRV Associations, PO Box 1364, Honoka'a, HI 96727
Phone: (808) 990-3354
e-mail: srvinfo@srv.org   website: www.srv.org
Nectar Subscription is on a donation basis only

No part of this publication may be reproduced or transmitted in any form without permission from the publisher. Entire contents copyright 2020. All Rights Reserved. ISSN 1531-1414

Editor
Babaji Bob Kindler

Associate Editor
Annapurna Sarada

Production
Lokelani Kindler

Cover Image:
Annapurna Sarada

Acknowledgement
*Image of Ramakrishna's Disciples
Courtesy of Vedanta Press
800-816-2242*

Contributing Writers
Swami Aseshananda
Swami Brahmeshananda
Swami Sunirmalananda
Lam FuHo
Rabbi Rami Shapiro
Sheikh Nur al-Jerrahi
Annapurna Sarada
Brother Tadrupa
Babaji Bob Kindler

EDITORIAL

In the Upanisads there is a wonderful sloka on the nature of bliss in the world, given out by the ancient rishis of India during an auspicious period of higher awareness and achievement. It relates that "....the crops are showering Bliss upon us, our works are showering Bliss upon us, our children are showering Bliss upon us," etc. It was an age of truth and dharma, to be sure.

This is much the way I feel about the *Nectar of Nondual Truth* magazine, now in your hands and available for close scrutiny. SRV makes the effort to publish it in written form so that the Bliss contained within human intelligence can emerge and be savored. In other words, in the hands and minds of awakened souls, these articles will shower Bliss upon the reader, transporting each individual to a unique and transcendent position that is beyond the reach of the ordinary mind and impervious to the influence of the world's constant plagues and catastrophes. Is it escapism? If it is, it is of the type that confers fulfillment and aids divine souls in accomplishing all works in the world in a safe and karma-free spirit.

So then, let us escape for a few hours into the radiant and inwardly redolent realm of the Wisdom Mother, and just lay, unreservedly, in Her womb of contemplative Peace; there we can relish the Truth, uninterruptedly. In Her endearing and nonpareil atmosphere all errors are forgiven, all ignominies are neutralized, all misunderstandings are healed, and all trespasses are forgiven — particularly those involving humanity's short-sighted vision concerning the innate unity of the world's religious traditions. Enough of controversy — emotional, social, political, psychological, scientific, religious, philosophical — as if it were the only occupation and state of mind that a human being should take up....as if we are to push to a distance the Great Ones and the pure and ignorance-destroying teachings of the Eternal Dharma that, when contemplated free of the mind posited in criticism and polluted by calumny, confer real and actual Bliss upon us.

In the scriptures of India it is said that the heart's devotion to the Lord is its own fruit. The same must be said about the mind's phases of knowledge and wisdom, leading to Truth. Lower knowledge, *aparavidya*, will never free the soul bound in the physical frame, suffering in these repetitive cycles amidst the inevitable decay of matter. As Swami Vivekananda has stated, "....it will only satisfy the soul for a short time." Further, as Sri Krishna relates, "....it will lead to danger if it is not connected to and aligned with Truth." Our Western society today, if not the entire ensuing world, is certainly an example of both of these statements, which should then become hearkened warnings for the soul seeking true freedom along the singular path leading to Enlightenment.

In a recent issue of Nectar of Nondual Truth (Issue #30), I composed an article called *Mumukshutvam*, which means the deep yearning for Freedom that is unalloyed and unmixed with any other desire. Who has it? When we saw, heard of, or read about the life of Sri Ramakrishna Paramahamsadeva, we beheld it. Was His mind always concerned about individual financial welfare, worried over the menial concerns of daily family life, stressed out about jobs and the vaunted security they pretend to confer? Was it continually laboring amidst mind-imbalancing controversies, or vexing about the constant flow of the surface changing phenomena around Him? Was he even afraid on the imminence of death? Free of all and sundry, life, Eternal Life, simply showered Bliss upon Him. He was, as our SRV founder, Lex Hixon, often related, as stated in his profound book, *Great Swan*, "A true human being....."

Free the mind first; the body will follow naturally. In the nondual scriptures it is related, "Ignorance is unreal, so how can it cause you any real doubt? What, then, does the yogi do with the mind and its projections? He lets them all rise spontaneously, then dissolves them into the Ocean of Consciousness at the end of each day — like bubbles into water."

Babaji in Vrindavan

Om Peace, Peace, Peace
Babaji Bob Kindler

NECTAR OF ADVAITIC INSTRUCTION

Questions from Our Readers

The hosts of questions concerning spiritual life and practice, along with the problems and issues it raises, is an important part of inner growth, even if often spiced with frankness and controversy. Nevertheless, teachers of the dharma are present and always on the spot to offer apt clarification.

"I just finished reading *Bhakti Yoga* and *Karma Yoga* by Swami Vivekananda, as you advised. How do we reconcile each of these yogic paths, or is there no need to? I feel any practice one follows would be a perfect mix of all of them."

Yes, it is true. But following one's practice after having made all the right connections is superior to just letting things fall into place over time, for time can meddle with even the best-intentioned sadhana, as we all know.

Philosophically, the Four Yogas of Jnana, Bhakti, Raja, and Karma, are intrinsically one. When practice of them ensues, however, depending upon the varying temperaments and karmas of any given practitioner, it is often necessary to focus in on one in order to "raise one up by one's bootstraps," as they say. This is true because souls have made more progress along one avenue in a past lifetime than along others. Thus, when the present lifetime appears to them, they are already imbued with certain abilities that will aid them in coping with new life and growth. It is the more advanced soul, spiritually speaking, who have made inroads into two or even more of the four main yogic pathways, i.e., action, wisdom, devotion, and contemplation/meditation. These are rather marvelous to behold, as they integrate all manner of qualities and capabilities into the phenomenal picture.

Regarding the bhakti and karma paths, as you mention, devotion in action and action with devotion, however one wants to put it, smooths the way to enlightenment considerably. What Vivekananda speaks of in these two books accomplishes both the individual's guidance along each avenue, and introduces the possibility of finding a way to dovetail the two into a more consummate way of proceeding towards Freedom, Moksha/Mukti.

And so, they may not need reconciliation, at least not for the intelligent aspirant, but they will require interior knowledge of the workings of each in order that the cogs on the belt of each can fit together and pull the body/mind vehicle successfully along the road of life, and into Eternal Life. As Sri Ramakrishna has stated in this regard: *"There is a special machine called the psycho/physical body. If the mechanic shows up every day to add oil into this mechanism, then all runs smoothly and the machine accomplishes all its functions. That oil is called devotion to God. If the machine does not receive its daily dose of oil, then it will soon seize up, break down, and fail in all undertakings thereafter."*

"It's interesting what we talked about concerning mental obstacles in our recent exchange. I have seen similar things with my students in an experimental class that we are running in college. It's really been revealing how deep the obstacles can run into their consciousness and mechanisms. They can wake up for a few days, or weeks, and then go right back to their bad habits without even noticing. Sometimes I think it is nothing short of a miracle to be where I am at. The conclusion that has come is that this Shakti power you transmit, that manifests as the will to do what is necessary to gain control and live less attached to limited thinking, is to be revered. It's simply amazing. And related, I think I finally understand some of things that are necessary for a leader to do who has a standard to hold in order to preserve the integrity of whatever sector they lead in. And the dharma teachers have to have the highest standards, and thus the most difficult job. I think true leaders who have this kind of integrity who are out there and visible, are so misunderstood and criticized as a result. I think it has been nearly lost in the Western World. Any thoughts on this? Anyways, it's starting to make more and more sense why the gurus are the way they are."

If there is anything on this earth to worship, of a formless and underlying nature, it is Shakti. Salutations to Her, and salutations to the Formless Brahman. I am glad that you have opened the inner eye to see, and keep up the process — until all processes end in Her.

Guru has been lost, as you say, to the Western world, because it was never very present in the first place — not in any prevalent or worshipful way. The church took over that role. Besides that, just look at the mishmash of gurus that are now on the scene here on earth, all vying for fame and money, and devoid of any dharma, or its accent. Various websites are shameful displays of this indiscriminate admixture. How can the Self be realized here and today if there is no exemplar for It? And how to even begin without a method, and a teacher for it?

Wend your way as straight as possible. Steer clear of charlatans. Follow the razor's-edged path that is discernible by its rarity and subtlety, and by the very few who adhere to it in this world and lifetime."

"The recent SRV retreat was definitely beneficial for my practice. I feel more connected to Divine Mother than before, and more confident that my practice is having a positive effect. I feel that I am worthy of experiencing Divine Reality. What else can I do to increase this type of forward progress?"

This is a good question to ask, and everyone should be asking it daily about their respective spiritual lives. Forget about the usual doubts, fears, insecurities, and lack of confidence, and just ask this question and engage in the superlative practices that spiritual life, true life, here on earth is all about.

In other words, resting upon one's laurels is seldom a good idea. Holy Mother has advised us not to try and measure our spiritual progress, as this will increase vanity and/or also usher in its opposite, doubt about the validity of real inner growth.

At the same time we are to observe the positive effects of sadhana well-accomplished under the guidance of the spiritual preceptor, and in the company of other like-minded devotees. If our witness consciousness gets ahold of such positive benefits, the path forward then becomes strewn with the fragrant rose petals of burgeoning spiritual experiences, whereas if the ego latches onto the same, then the constant back and forth of the duality of "good for me" and "I am worthless" tends to set into the mind.

This explains some of the dynamics of Advaita Vedanta Sadhana, as contrasted to what dharma teachers sometimes indicate as "goal-oriented sadhana." For, it is true that the Soul knows everything already, that the Essence of mankind is perfect. Here on earth, however, where the mayic veil has come down hard and thick over the individual mind, the better route and attitude to take is the one of subjecting the ego to practices that will thin out said veil and help reveal the light of higher understanding behind it. Constant revelation rather than recurring regression will then become the standard for spiritual life, leading to the certitude of authentic inner realization in stages.

"I am really enjoying the book, Self Knowledge. In particular I have had inspired laughter by the commentary where the author writes that Truth cannot be known through the mind, since mind itself is a product of ignorance. Very illuminating. Also, the Sanskrit term adhistana has been awesome in explaining what the seers mean by substratum. Are kutashta and adhistana synonymous? AUM."

Adhisthana and Kutastha are verisimilar. They are both words for Brahman. The latter epithet emphasizes the unmoving aspect of Brahman, what is often called "Rock-Seated." The former word zeroes in on Brahman's subtlety by way of background Consciousness, Its presence as The Support for everything. The differences are indeed subtle, but also helpful to know

"In the past I have seen myself making some spiritual progress, but over time I then noticed that I had slipped back and lost the ground that I gained. At the same time, but only later, did I see that attachments I thought I had mastered had returned on me and gotten back into my life. I now doubt my own ability to turn things around, spiritually. It is disheartening to see maya so easily overturn my best intentions. How do I keep going forward in this disappointing atmosphere?"

One must learn to value the unseen qualities of spiritual life, and place the obvious pleasures and surface attainments of life behind them. That is why Jesus stated to *"Seek the Kingdom of Heaven first and foremost, and the world thereafter." Also, "Store up your treasures in heaven, not just on earth."* Practice this unique state of mind and attitude a little and the rest will come to you in due time. *"If thine eye offend thee, then cut it out,"* was how Jesus put this. This means that the eye that only notices base, changing, and menial things ought to be plucked out and replaced by the "Third Eye of Wisdom."

To be successful at this you will need to destroy doubt, for it stops one in their tracks before they even get going — as you now know. So work on putting doubt away, then take to deeper and higher things."

"'Shiva destroys ignorance,' is what you wrote to me. But the root center opens first, and the Third Eye is at an extremely high level. When I was given mantra, I got a glimpse of losing the world. The best way I can describe this is that I feel like sometimes I am "in the world, but not of the world." This only happened after you gave me my Mantra. Therefore, is this not part of the third eye peeking, per se,' and some of the world getting destroyed? You mentioned that a student once said that you 'destroyed his life.' Isn't this like a destroyed part of the world, by seeing through a spiritual eye, or third eye? Disciples are able to experience this by a guru handing down a mantra to a student. Is this not what happened when you activated and transmitted me my mantra? I mean, no ordinary man can do that to another."

The sixth center, Lotus, or "Chakra," is a very deep level of Consciousness wherein the soul will see the Light of Brahman, hear the sound of AUM, and connect with the highest of all Deities — like Sri Ramakrishna.

And you are absolutely right, that one must awaken the Kundalini Shakti, Divine Mother Power, from the root chakra inwards, or upwards, prior to the opening of this "Third Eye." One does that via the sacred mantra repeated constantly, the reading of spiritual books and scriptures, and various devotions of worship as well. As the process deepens, occasionally the aspirant will gain a glimpse of higher centers, but still not be able to abide in them yet.

Siva destroys ignorance in the mind, where all worlds exist. At the end of a Cosmic Cycle (yuga) He will "destroy" all worlds, reducing them back to their seed essence as causal thought in the Cosmic Mind.

Levels of Consciousness, and consciousness itself, align with the seven chakras. Most outer and heavenly states of consciousness operate at the three lowest chakras. When the individual surrenders to the Lord and Mother, the fourth chakra opens, and real Love is discovered. This can happen even in this world, when devout souls find one another. All other love is either fake, or limited, or temporary.

"What should one expect on the spiritual path? What should be the objective one should strive for on this path?"

In this day and age, the best an average working person can expect from their spiritual life is daily practice, i.e., sadhana. Sadhana has to be maintained at all times, and under all circumstances. The positive effects of it, such as peace of mind, will appear later down the line, but one has to keep it up constantly in the meantime. With a good spiritual practice in place, then the Ideal of Moksha, or Enlightenment, can be practically and effectively sought after.

"Studying the Raja Yoga lessons, I find that my mind is always kshipta. How can I get to the stages of controlled mind?"

One gets there by taking a part of the mind and clearing it of obstacles. If one can make a part of the mind clear, then the rest can be worked on later, and with more ease. At first this is hard work. As the song in India relates, *"O Mind: you are a jungle of under-growth, out of control. I intend to take a machete and cut out and clear an acre, and on that acre I will build a temple to Divine Mother. Then I can go there for peace and rest. I can then clear the rest of the acres later."*

"In my past I have come in contact with and been damaged psychically by false teachers/gurus. I would have given up the spiritual path by now except that something inside of me drives me on. Some of us are so grateful to have found you, and SRV. What do you advise for those of us in this unenviable position of 'psychic damage'?"

It is very good that you have prevailed, even against such odds, and are trying to follow through with that inner yearning for enlightenment. As you go forward in this manner, you will want to analyse the paths and teachers that are coming forward in your life, and stay clear of paths that accent hatha yoga, paths which allow the use of intoxicants as a part of their practices, and ones that proceed by miracles and sensational promises. There are books out there, like autobiographies by sensationalists, whose pages are filled with occult powers. Such displays come from the spiritual ego, which is to be avoided.

Shankara has given the standard for the sincere seeker who wants to remain clear of charlatans. The real guru will possess akamahata (having no other desire than the student reach freedom), avrigina (sporting the will to live a pure and simple life), shrotriya (knowing and being able to transmit the essence of the scriptures), and Brahamvid (is a knower of Divine Reality). Check all gurus against this measure, and you will find your way.

"What profound belief and convictions have you had while you were on this path? What would you suggest for me to believe in as I embark on this journey?"

Seeing my guru and taking teachings with him were very convincing. I was already seeking sincerely at the age of 20, so I made swift progress in his divine atmosphere. I also came to knowledge of Sri Ramakrishna and Holy Mother at an early age. Reading about and hearing about Their divine lives was another aid to my deeper convictions. Everyone should read the Gospel of Sri Ramakrishna as a help to their deepest convictions.

"What is the role of faith, and what causes the shaking of one's faith in higher reality? How should a seeker keep faith strong until the goal is reached? How can we ensure that the journey is complete, and there is no halting or midway escape?"

The faith of beginning aspirants after truth today gets shaken by bad parental examples, by not getting the dharma given at an early age, by society's adoption of violence and greed, by the fall of religion in this day and age, by the violent military posture that countries take, and by the rush of people everywhere to gain pleasure through objects, etc. This is the Kali Yuga, with its ills and allurements. One must offset it by taking teachings from an illumined soul, reading the scriptures, worshipping the deities, and doing all work as worship as far as is possible. One's faith should always and ever be in God, not in the world.

"I really think our satsang yesterday has brought light on a lot of the teachings about Practical Vedanta and Monistic Vedanta practiced under an illumined guru. I had mentioned months ago about not knowing how to properly digest this Shiva-principle in action with the idea of being steady and strong in one's conviction, and not depending on or compromising with others. It is even starting to get clear about how certain Western principles and philosophies like rugged individualism, and like we mentioned yesterday, Transcendentalism; they have some good points, but lack the important psychological understanding of seership. I was reading a little more about Emerson's philosophy. He believed in an all-pervasive Divine Consciousness, and that each soul was inherently connected to It. He also denounced the church. He was even a minister. Some of his colleagues clearly expressed that their inspiration came from the Upanisads and Gita. As we discussed, he encourages use of intuition to guide one's speech and actions, and also emphasizes nonconformity in order to stay true to what one feels is right. I think they were limited, though, because they didn't seek or have access to direct counsel from a living seer to know in a very personal way that there are those whom you can depend upon, and who can make intuition clear and totally reliable, i.e. illumined buddhi. Perhaps this missing link in their philosophy is the reason why it did not take wider appeal."

This analysis is very good. You are delving deeper and deeper towards the essence of real life and living, being one of the few, even one of the pioneers (still) that have taken up the ideal and the teachings that Swami Vivekananda brought here to America and are putting them into practice. I pray fervently that you will only persevere in this endeavor, for if you do, the Mother of the Universe will very definitely aid you in reaching what Swami Vivekananda has called, *"The true Goal of human existence."*

"While contemplating this latest Mother Kali poem you sent, I thought of fractals — infinitely complex patterns that continue to reveal additional detail as one examines them in progressively closer frames of reference. Similarly, I'm sure there is much more to understand in this poem, just like in other poems you have sent me, and other wisdom scriptures, but I think I am ready to look at another, so please send one. I am adamant that I should remain faithful to guru, mantra, and practice, so that I can be a good example for my children, since my wife and I have just had our first baby."

Excellent that you are studying in this manner, and especially that you are working on your spiritual life to keep it alive and well, despite or even in the press of having just had a baby. What else is life for, and how can it fulfill us if, even just for our children's sake, there is no spiritual activity and realization in it?

"'Practice of Yoga brings bad experiences as well, which are also important.' Could you please elaborate on this statement of yours in the recent Raja Yoga lesson you sent me?"

Negative teachings are what I mean to say, like "....*what is sour in the beginning, but sweet later on,*" as Sri Krishna states. The neti neti style of Vedanta that wants the aspirant to disidentify with the world, the ego, the senses, and their objects — these are called negative teachings. To get peace one must detach from the world of mundane habits and surface goings-on. Spending time in deep study and meditation is good for gaining some peace of mind.

Additionally, "bad experiences" come in the form of past negative karmas of the past (this lifetime and the last) that surface when the sincere practitioner engages in serious sadhana. Hopefully, these will not cause the aspirant to give up on the spiritual path, and the mantra that often brings these hidden devils to the surface of the mind for purification.

"**Bhakti and Karma Yoga first, before getting into Jnana Yoga, is your suggestion. Babaji, please tell me about these two first, and how I should establish myself in these before I start the practice of Raja Yoga.**"

Actually, I would prefer that people got dharmic knowledge first, then underwent work and worship; but that works only for people who have already attained the ability to comprehend the scriptures and perceive the importance of Atmajnana. One should attend upon a qualified teacher to focus on Jnanam.

But if you read carefully Swami Vivekananda's books entitled *Karma Yoga* and *Bhakti Yoga,* and ask questions, that will be very good for your acquisition of higher knowledge.

The reason I have been absent from retreats is due to schooling and family. I'm frustrated with how the timing of events in this life are working out. On one hand, my mother and grandmother desperately need help, so I've been helping them. They are, as Sri Ramakrishna has quipped about worldly families, 'a pit of vipers.' I want to help them, but at the same time I know that I cannot. Sometimes I don't know exactly why I feel so attached/obligated to them. So, the past two weekends I've been with the vipers/family. The level of chaos and suffering that is present there is hard to deal with. I feel like the world is in my way, and it is also in the way of me and the sangha, and purity of mind. I've spent 38 hours of the last 3 days on homework, and wrote well over 1000 lines of code, experiencing all kinds of ups and downs. As I was reading the lab rubric later at night, I realized that I had misinterpreted part of the instruction resulting in a phenomenally late night, which taught me a very valuable and insightful lesson in organization and planning. After rewriting/restructuring about 70% of my code that night, and writing a very honest, thorough, and concise lab report today, when I submitted all the work I found that the entire report was actually a day late. This was a crushing blow when I found out. School matters to me, and I'm taking a remarkably heavy load this summer. It probably wouldn't be so bad if my family was not in dire need of help, but I do know that it feels right to some extent to help them. I feel like the world is eating me alive right now. I have never felt more overwhelmed with school, family, bills etc. And I feel bad as a spiritual aspirant that I'm so late, or absent, for classes/retreat. I wish I could be in class, see you and the rest of the Sangha, because I know it would help. It sounds lame for me say, but the past two or three weeks its been hard to keep my head above water."

This diatribe from you on the time-consuming nature of the materially-oriented world is becoming common to hear from the youth of today — what youth out there who are still interested in spiritual life and its salient concerns. I am including it here in Nectar in its entirety so that people may read and get a deeper perspective on this ever-increasing problem in our nation, and also in the world at large. Without basic peace of mind, what to speak of time to pursue the essential achievements of life such as meditation and enlightenment of mind, not only will the quality of life in our world continue to rapidly decline, but even sanity of mind may begin to erode.

So thank you for your frank and thorough description here. We miss you here as well, and are sending all love and support for you to get through that period of worldliness, i.e., family, school, etc. Keep the mantra, and Master and Holy Mother, in your heart and mind, and just push through it all. Try to come on retreat, setting that as a goal in advance and letting nothing get in the way.

Yes, serve your relatives, that "viper pit" with its dense layers of ignorance. Do what you can for them, but keep a part of yourself free and away. For now, your juggling act is with three balls — family, schoolwork, and spiritual life. Strive for a balance. The trial will be good for you in the long run, building strength and perseverance.

Further, all that I can advise at this time, you and I being presently distant from one another in location, is to recite the mantra daily and try to convert all work into worship. The main reason that I give the mantra to my students — the one I received from my own guru during sacred ceremony on Holy Mother's birthday — is so that they will be prepared, even saved, when such concentrated periods of descending karmas come crashing down on them in the midst of life and activity. A better scenario would be if I could give the mantra to them during a time and period where they could go within and spend quality time reflecting upon it. But alas.....

For those who are working in the world, and who seek what society, schooling, and upbringing encourage as the goal of human existence, other forces are at work. To survive these forces is to keep one's nose above the waters of worldliness just long enough to allow a period of peace and quiet to descend. Otherwise, if it does not, one must force the hand of maya and cause it to happen by one's own sweet will. Incredibly enough, there are people — even young people — who are doing just that, and thereby wending their way through the world-bewitching maya to find the Eternal Peace that lies, always and ever, behind it. God-speed to you, and to all, in this effort to go beyond all darkness to the farthest Shore. Peace x's 3

"**It was good that we had another chance to talk about the dharma recently! It is also helpful to have in mind that we already are the Atman, and at the same time have the capacity to practice sadhana. It gives one the chance to overcome one's shortcomings. Lately I have been aspiring to live a more** balanced lifestyle, but I would like to conserve more energy to do spiritual practices and not end up tired by the end of the day. I have also been inspecting your teachings; I would like to rediscover again and again the profundity of your teachings, and remain inspired on this level. I think this is a facet of what Sattvic balance is. There are many things that are complicating my worldly life. I would like to gain more responsibility in being practical in life, and I think that this will help with my forgetfulness, too. I mean this also in regards to handling money well, dealing with objects better, to a point where I can leave a part of my mind on God."

Yes, for the householder it is a matter of holding fast to Brahman while doing one's duties in a detached spirit. And by keeping contact with the spiritual teacher a great amount of benefit can be had as well, and a great amount of trouble can also be avoided. It is rather like taking up residence in a house with a contemplative instead of living in a house with a tiger. Trouble is bound to happen in the latter case.

As to us already being the Atman, I wish it were true. That is, it is true, literally, but all seekers must learn the rare art of conscious Awareness of this fact based upon personal realization, and not just speak it with the lips, or even merely entertain it with the mind. Until then, it would be better to tell ourselves that we are not Atman until we that realize we are Atman, and thus avoid more tiger-like trouble — on the philosophical level.

"I have contemplated your teachings on the 8 Yamas of Yoga Regarding ahimsa, though I am non-violent physically, I tend to show contempt towards people in my thoughts. I have dislikes and prejudice toward people, and I hate people who block my path. I sometimes speak ill of others. I tend to be harsh and rude at times. I can't put up with insults, rebukes, and criticism. I hold intense feelings of retaliation and taking revenge. I tend to offend people right there and then when I am being offended. Finally, I never forget and forgive. Please help me to establish myself in Ahimsa."

All of the things you cite above are problems in the ego, ahamkara. They are painful facets of human nature today. One must work on them using observance of the yamas and niyamas so as to minimize such behaviors and ways of negative thinking. If a person does not want to be under their influence anymore, then such a one will change human nature via constant practice (abhyasa yoga) and become an all-around better person, returning once again to their divine nature. For more help on this, read scripture and ask questions of the guru, attend retreats, meditate daily for peace of mind and balance, and practice compassion for the sufferings of others. Others are suffering these very things you describe herein. Help them to help themselves, and you will find that help also comes your way.

"Today I was reading from the Nectar magazine about Lex Hixon's pilgrimage on the Haj. I really liked how spontaneous he was in speaking to the people of New York on the radio. My friend is a Hindu, and really does not like Islam, mainly because they eat meat. I could not really be very convincing on the subject, being vegetarian myself. For myself, however, I have to deepen in one particular path, and I am willing to do that. I see that people might benefit more in deepening themselves in one particular path, but I can't see how deep one must go before one can open to other perspectives. But I shouldn't question this; I will see for myself if I can just make the move, and dive deeper. It is of great help to me that I am gaining strength in the fact that you are my guru."

Narrowness invades every mind, and all religious perspectives, I'm afraid. Just look at this as beings passing through a necessary phase of narrow thinking, which will help them to concentrate on one particular path and perspective until such a time as sweet Universality visits the mind. At the early juncture of spiritual striving the immature aspirant cannot see the mountain through the forest, or even the forest through the trees. Later, some of the most limited of people often turn into the most wide and catholic beings alive. It is one of the greatest of miracles, really.

So in the meantime you can look with awe at people like Lex Hixon, whose high-minded stature was an ideal to all who came in contact with him, whether they liked him in the end or not. He did what he knew to be best for all who were involved with him. If this were not true, then you never would have read about true Islam, and would not even be reading the words of this journal, a unique and rare magazine that was inspired by him, if it were not for his shining life and excellent example.

"Why is the spiritual path referred to as 'razor's-edged'?"

Those of us who tread this unique path should know that by now, since we have attempted it and are finding it very hard. And the hardships along it are different than those of the worldly path. Spirituality is really a matter of subtleties, not of worldly affairs. Spiritual fruits are entirely different than earthly ones. That is why one must "....*store them up in Heaven.*" The followers of the path of Light must learn to seek the unseen treasures, then place them first in order of importance, relegating the worldly fruits thereafter. Success along the razor's-edged path is mostly a matter of priorities, then. It is a *"Seek Thee First"* kind of method and procedure.

"Recently I read where you wrote in the Raja Yoga lessons, 'Remain steady and unaffected in the midst of good and bad, praise and blame, honor and dishonor, and pleasure and pain. This is critical to the attainment of the unique fruits of spirituality.' But I am so far away from this ideal state of being. Can I ever achieve it? Doubt arises often, and any glimpse of this high state leaves me frightened, and as a result I walk away from the path in order to get some comfort and relief from that feeling. Please help me in understanding my fear, and to get established in this ideal state."

Fear is one of the obstacles, to be sure. Doubt in oneself, and in the teachings and the teacher, is another. From these two spring the confused mind's brooding on the unreal, which will then eventually fashion the unreal into its own perverse idea of reality and thereafter live dully in it, deluded, even for lifetimes.

That is why you have quoted me saying here what are really the words and advice of Sri Krishna in the Gita. These sets of dualities assail the mind trapped in maya, so that the only recourse of the wise and far-seeing person is to gain stability — even if it means giving up the world and all its pallid purposes and puerile people and starting over again, with God only.

I used to hear my guru, Swami Aseshanandaji, state, from the podium, in his lectures, *"Through surging waves and changing tides, One Light guides."* And he should know, coming from a far distant country as a world-renouncing sannyasin to try and teach the very essence of stability in life, called Vedanta, to Americans — who, by the way are, for the most part, the very epitome of instability and fearfulness, with sizable amounts of uncertainty, noncommitment, and waywardness mixed in. They have made a weird artform out of running away from the Light of God and burying themselves deeper, and deeper still, into the very principle of decaying matter. If one tries to help them out, they snap at the hand that would assist them and, in their arrogance, think that they know better than the knowers of Truth. *"Grasping matter, losing Grace, strange indeed this human race...."*

True stability is the world-destroying Wisdom that is called stithi prajnasya in the Gita, and the Lord, there, advises it again and again to all beings who stand on the battlefield of birth and death, and worthless worldly life, seeking a Peace that not only *"passeth all understanding,"* but also escapes even intellectual minds bound in maya's chains. If you are desiring it, yearning for it, which it sounds as if you very definitely are, then give up all manner of other things to secure it. The world will stand in your way — parents, family, education, society, military, job, and invisible but still present ancestors — but all of these can be cast aside for Peace. The only real blockage in your way to having it as your own is your own human mind. Therefore, work with your mind using Raja Yoga — the study of which has already brought up this question, and this yearning, from your mind.

"I am writing to you after watching the classes on the Akshi Upanisad on live-streaming. I am very greatful to be listening to them. It is truly like holy company for me; it is like being present there with you. So much that you say holds relevance in my life, and today, especially, I felt that you were guiding me through maya — for, the last couple of days has been hard for me. To help myself I have been practicing pratipakshabhavanam so as to bring out whatever good I have in my life. I want to settle more and more into steady wisdom, knowing that the soul never dies. What is it that keeps me from knowing myself, and recognizing what to overcome, like which of the six passions are more predominant in my life, and what triggers them? I would not only like to get glimpses of my true nature, but would like to live continuously in it — something that I haven't yet accomplished. I think its important to gather all my strength and channel it into one path. This will clear away a lot of ignorance and I can then make headway. But all that you say has got me thinking that this knowledge is already there within me, so why am I wanting to gain something which I already have? Is Jnana Yoga really like that, that you are realizing something that is already yours, and that you don't have to go out searching for it? But in the same way, you might be apt to assume that it is easy to obtain, because it is already yours. I would also like to be more patient in my practice, for that is one thing that I haven't been able to do, that is, master my sadhana. I think I would be able to conserve my energy better if I could gain the capability to wait out negative karmas and gunas. However, when I reflect, I see that I don't think that I am nothing less than I ever was. The realizations that I had previously in my sadhana are ever mine, and I can recall them if I so choose to do so. My memory is really good in this regard."

A good, resilient, and retentive memory is almost as good, and as coveted by the wise, as a pure mind. It is this powerful memory, referred to as smriti-hetu in the scriptures of India, which gives one many of the "glimpses," as you say here, of the radiant realm of the Spirt. Obversely, it is also the lack of it that causes the wonders of Divine Reality — Brahman, Ishvara, The Word, The Trinity, Divine Mother Shakti — to abandon human consciousness, leaving it dead and lifeless in the end. Lamentably, for the worldly-minded who are devoid of retentive memory, and who try to replace it with insipid sentimentality, consciousness was always dead; never really lived.

And you ask about Jnana Yoga. It is the swiftest and most effective way of burning out karmas that impede spiritual progress. Then, one can see what is already and always their own, but not until. Merely waiting for one's karmas to surface is far inferior than ferreting them out of hiding utilizing sadhana, and doing away with them on the spot, in this lifetime.

"Thank you for the further teachings/transmission. In my study of Sankhya philosophy, are you suggesting that I pursue it on my own? If so, could you please direct me to the study textbook I can refer to for the same?"

Sankhya is a very ancient system, and none, if any substantial scriptures, are available for it. If you begin to watch some of my Youtube classes, or the live-streaming classes of SRV, you will begin to pick up a lot of the wisdom of Sankhya. Also, ask specific questions regarding Lord Kapila's system, just as you are doing with the Raja Yoga studies we are undertaking together.

For, though ancient and rare of hearing, Sankhya has influenced so many of India's best and brightest philosophical systems. Thankfully for us living in this late age, it was so powerful and convincing that it penetrated into the fabric of other systems, like Yoga, Vedanta, and Shaivism. One can absorb it, then, by studying these and others.

"About satyam, I find that speaking out the facts to others sometimes annoys them; people do not like to listen to the truth, not even the relative truth. And so I 'lie' sometimes to save myself from the trouble, and sometimes to please others, and sometimes to avoid awkward situations. How can this be satyam? Please help me to establish myself in Satya."

Telling a lie so as to avoid hurting others is not really lying. One cannot just go around pointing out people's shortcomings with harsh words. It will make matters worse in most instances. So practice ahimsa by using soothing words, and that will be in line with satyam. In cases where people open themselves up for deeper instruction, one can relate the truth of the matter — still using gentle words which help a person change for the better.

Questions, observations and insights regarding problems in spiritual life or the issues of the day may be directed to Nectar's editorial staff at srvinfo@srv.org and will be duly answered in succeeding issues.

◆ *SRV Staff*

HEARING VEDANTA
Let's Not Get Lost in Translation

Teachers of Vedanta, as well as intermediate and advanced practitioners, necessarily stretch or redefine words in English to serve as vehicles for spiritual and philosophical terms in Sanskrit. The wonderful catholicity of Vedanta also shapes and reshapes the speaker's or writer's own understanding of the English words they are using, so that they often forget how most English speakers are still using those words. It has been said that "in order to be understood, one needs to understand." That is, one needs to understand the meaning behind the words another is using, and also how they will understand the words oneself are using. We need to "be on the same page," figuratively and quite literally. To this end, the following are explanations of English words adapted for use in Vedanta.

Spirit, Soul, Spiritual, Spirituality

In Vedanta, Spirit (with a capital "S") is used to express That which is not made of matter, and not just atomic matter, but also energy and thought. In Indian cosmology, physical matter, energy, mind, and thought are all gross or subtle forms of matter limited by time and space. Spirit is uncaused, transcendent and imminent, and pre-exists everything. Being eternal, and transcending/pervading everything else, It is "one without a second." When It is lower-cased, it refers to the individual's subtle self, a combination of energy, mind, intellect, and ego that supports the physical body and then transmigrates after the body dies. Spirit and spirit are often used interchangeably with Soul and soul. In Sanskrit, the word is *Atman*. Or it can be the pair: *Paramatman* (supreme indivisible Self) and *Jivatman* (the *Atman* modified by energy, mind, intellect, and ego/*ahamkara*).

Thus, the terms spiritual and spirituality, in Vedanta, refer to ideas, teachings, practices, lifestyles, etc., that emphasize Spirit/Soul and one's identification with It. For instance, a "spiritual life" would consist of practices that purify the mind (as opposed to efforts at purifying the body) so that one can identify with the Spirit/Atman and relegate everything else to the category of vehicles or reflectors of Spirit. Merely feeling healthy, happy, or temporarily blissful, are not spirituality but experiences in the various vehicles of body, mind, intellect, and ego. "Turn emotion into devotion" – spiritual practices like worship, study, and meditation sublimate ordinary emotions into higher forms so that mere bliss is finally transcended for eternal Bliss (which is the nature of Spirit/Atman, along with Existence, and Awareness).

God

It is tempting to forego using this perfectly good Divine Name due to the reactions that so many "religion-refugees" have to It. But let's not. When Vedantists use this word, it does not mean a bearded, judgmental man sitting on a throne in a heaven somewhere. Hopefully, that conception represents only a small share of religionists, despite its resilient depictions in Western culture. Rather, Vedantists use it is a general word for Divine Reality, inclusive of both a personal, approachable Aspect that is the sum total of all beneficent, divine qualities (*Ishvara* or *Saguna Brahman*), and also the Ultimate Impersonal Reality that is non-dual (*Nirguna Brahman*). Sanskrit conveniently has special terms for each Aspect, but in English, Vedantists often make do with "the Personal God" (with or without a gender; with or without a form) and "Impersonal God." "*Advaita Vedantists focus on the Impersonal*," one Vedantic teacher explains, "*but they do not de-personalize It.*" That is, God resides within the subtle heart as the Highest Divine Personality, or at the deepest core of our Consciousness as our own Supreme Self.

Religion, religion

Religion is another word that raises the hackles of some people. Swami Vivekananda helped us understand its meaning, and we should not lose the memory of that. He made a distinction between Religion, upper-cased, and religion lower-cased. The first, Religion, refers to the particular teachings given by the great founders of religion and countless sages, which transcend geographical location and time, that is, those teachings that are true regardless of changing times and circumstances. The Sanskrit for this is *Sanatana Dharma* – the Eternal Religion, or Truth. These teachings are concerned with the nature of the Soul, the nature of God in Its two Aspects (personal/impersonal; with form or formless), the relationship between the individual Soul and God, and the nature of the world.

When religion is lower-cased, it refers to particular religions and their teachings given on a general level to their respective adherents, usually dualistic (God, beings, and world are all separate from each other) often with cultural, social, economic and political ramifications. The universal aspect of Religion is still there, no doubt, but takes a back seat or is fully concealed by these temporal issues, except in the cases of those practitioners yearning to see God, to realize God. Religion and religion coexist in all traditions. In Sanskrit the words for this are: *Sanatana Dharma* (the Eternal Religion) and *Yuga Dharma* (the religion for a particular age and region). According to Indian Philosophy and Religion, when the teachings of the religion of the age/region are in conflict with the Eternal Truths of Religion, then the latter is to take precedence. When that fails to happen, religion gets crystalized and dogmatic and goes into decline until a great Soul asserts the Eternal Truths of Religion again.

Pure, Purity, Purifying

When used Vedantically, the word "pure" signifies something that is unmixed. For instance, a "pure mind" is a mind that can contemplate the Self, Atman-Brahman, without getting distracted or modified by other thoughts. A pure mind merges naturally into its source, the Atman. The fact that it does not get distracted by earthly or self-centered thoughts and desires also means it is pure in the moral sense as well. This concept of "unmixed" is also essential for catching the essence of what is meant by expressions such as pure Awareness, pure Consciousness, pure Existence, pure Bliss or other similar statements. If it is unmixed, then it is the one eternal Source, for there can only be one eternal Reality. Thus, all these expressions are epithets for the One Without a Second. With regard to mind, Sri Ramakrishna has said that pure mind is God. That which is purifying, then, refers to practices that aid the practitioner in controlling the senses and mind so that the mind becomes concentrated and finally absorbed in God/the eternal Self.

Sin

Vedanta does not have a word that truly corresponds to "sin" in English. Probably few English words have to stretch so far to accommodate the original Sanskrit. People new to Vedanta are often relieved to find that Vedanta teaches Original Perfection as the root state of beings. But then we come across English translations of Sanskrit scriptures or hymns, and find "sin" being used. Admittedly this is jarring and confusing. The point to understand is that in Vedanta, the Soul/Atman/Spirit is impossible to taint. No finite action ever touches It, the Infinite, Eternal Self. It would be as if water could make space wet, or a sword could cleave space in two, to use analogies. However, selfish, violent, prideful, jealous, angry, hateful thoughts and actions do taint the mind and cause it to fall prey to guilt, dejection, remorse, and maybe cycles of deepening negative passions that lead to mental illness. Thus, when we see the word "sin" drafted into service, it is rather to encourage suffering people to make a change in their thoughts and actions, but always with the proviso that the Soul, the true Self, is ever pure, ever free – why wallow in self-inflicted, unnecessary mental anguish when Purity, Freedom, and Bliss are one's true nature? Knowing this up front is our refuge and strength for engaging in practices to purify the mind, preferably in the guiding and supportive company of *Guru*, *Dharma*, and *Sangha*.

Karma

This Sanskrit word has made its way into the English language and dictionaries. Very good definitions can be found regarding *karma* as the result of actions and how these are the cause of current and future births. Less known is *karma's* more basic meaning – action. Yes, *karma* means both action and its result(s), i.e. cause and effect. To focus on just the result leaves one in bondage to results, as if *karma* were a matter of predestination beyond one's control. Rather, the teachings on *karma* as cause and effect are meant to free us from both. It is not a matter of simply attempting to do good action in order to reap good *karmic* results; that is still bondage, "a gold chain." Acting in such a way that no *karmic* results accrue is one of the conditions of living in a state of Freedom. Thus, one should approach the scriptures (such as the *Bhagavad Gita*) and a qualified teacher to learn the dynamics of what is called *Karma Yoga*, the path of selfless action leading to Freedom and Illumination. Swami Vivekananda's little book, *Karma Yoga*, is an excellent first read on this topic.

Space, Sky, Ether

The Sanskrit word for which "space" is pulled into service is a deeply philosophical term. Knowledge of it (*akasha*) opens the gateway to awareness of subtle realities. English speakers think of it according to science, wherein space is affected by mass and gravity. When used Vedantically, space, sky, and ether all refer to 5 levels or dimensions, each more subtle than the last – all of which are all-pervasive at their level. For example, physical space, or the space of objects (*bhutakasha*), comes into existence before atomic/molecular objects can appear; it is the primal element, physically speaking. This space permeates all objects. When we move anything, space doesn't move or get displaced the way that air does. It is not made wet by water, heated by fire, dried by wind, or capable of being cut into two or many. It appears to be divided or modified (*upadhi*) by the objects that occupy it, but it is completely unaltered by them. It is something different from the space of science and physics, which is fine. Vedanta is describing something else.

It is important to be aware of this difference because Vedanta uses the insentient space of objects and its all-pervasive, unaffected, imminent and transcendent nature as an analogy to help people understand ultimate Reality - which is imminent and transcendent of all levels of space and is Sentiency itself, i.e., pure Conscious Awareness, according to the Indian Seers (past and current). It is the Great Support of all. The other levels of space are increasingly subtle and approached via the mind in meditation. In other words, after physical space, all other kinds of space are within: the space of energy (*pranakasha*), the space of thought (*chittakasha*), the space of Intelligence (*jnanakasha*), the space of pure Consciousness (*Chidakasha*), the ultimate Reality. These different kinds of space correspond to states of awareness the spiritual practitioner and adept enters via meditation and *samadhi* (the culmination of meditation).

Universe

Teachers of Vedanta often refer to the "universe of name and form." In common usage, "universe" means a physical realm of stars, planets, moons, black holes, comets, etc., and the space between them. In Indian cosmology, which informs most Indian schools of philosophy, "universe" is inclusive of not only the physical universe (*virat*), but fourteen strata of gross, subtle, and causal realms which all exist in the Cosmic Mind (*Mahat*), "cosmic" being used in the same expansive manner as "universe." These realms can be described as states of energy, thought, wisdom, as meaning, as pure dynamic Intelligence, and more. The beings inhabiting them are drawn to these various spheres according to their desires, spiritual attainments, and mental purity. Importantly, the minds of all beings in all strata are ultimately connected to the Cosmic Mind and each other, and through spiritual purification one can experience communion at these realms of awareness. However, to realize absolute Existence, Freedom, and Bliss as one's own nature, this Cosmic Mind and the universe of name and form must be transcended.

◆ Babaji Bob Kindler

KNOWING AFTER
The Insubstancial & Nonexistent Nature of Ignorance

Recently, and due to the need for brainstorming titles for a series of discourses to be given for SRV Associations in the year of 2019, one of the ideas for a series of talks that occurred to me was around the subject of the Six Proofs of Truth/Reality. Being a rather daunting prospect due to the complex and highly philosophical nature of the teaching, I deliberated for some time before including it into the host of Sunday Live-streaming classes for the year. As the time approached for actually giving the series live, I again wondered as to the wisdom of this choice — as well as about my capabilities to present such an abstruse nondual teaching.

The approach that saved me in the end was the decision to render the teaching along a more hands-on line, rather than a purely philosophical one, especially given that the subject had received many dry, intellectual treatments over time by pundits and scholars, placing it always in the atmosphere of argumentation and debate. To me, this always seemed counterproductive to the point, being the aim of cogently proving the existence of Brahman rather than merely speculating about it.

But surprisingly, and as a result of undertaking this abstruse subject matter, I later found out that the real benefit of it all had more to do with certain revelations given unto me, rather than clarity given unto others. This began with my consideration and contemplation of the very first proof of Truth (see chart on facing page), called *anumana*, or what is known in the tradition as "knowing after." In other words, one comes to know of certain bits of knowledge via inference. When beings implement inference with this rather hidden proof of Truth, they hardly notice that their ignorance around it goes away completely. This gets to the point of the insubstantially of all ignorance, really, and the utterly assumed nature of holding it in the mind at all.

"My Ignorance is Gone, Gone: Utterly Gone!"

Ignorance goes away because it was never there in the first place. As Sri Ramakrishna has stated in His *Gospel*, *"Like darkness laying inside of a cave for thousands of years, yet disappearing instantly when an explorer enters with a torch, just so does ignorance vanish in the revelatory light of knowledge."* Sri Krishna, in His *Bhagavad Gita*, states that *"The fire of knowledge is simply veiled by the smoke of ignorance — like an embryo is covered by the mother's womb. For that reason alone do beings suffer in darkness."*

The problem of appearances and the process of uncovering them fall to the one who tires of living with unnecessary limitations, and the suffering they cause. In not so ancient history, the *Advaitic-Shaivite Avatar*, Shankaracharya (around 700 A.D.), recovered most of his knowledge, gleaned from past lifetimes, at the tender age of 8, coming to remember much of what was contained in the Indian *darshanas* and their scriptures so as to dispense it once again, in that age, to sincere and deserving spiritual seekers. He was next heard of teaching grey-beards in his teens, and writing his commentaries on the *Bhagavad Gita* and some of the *Upanisads* in his 20's — what to speak of explanations on the truly abstruse *Brahma-Sutras*.

This thought, concept, idea, or fact of "knowing after," then, is sublime to contemplate. One might ask, then: was I ever truly ignorant? If this assumption of ignorance is a misfeasance perpetrated in the courtroom of *maya*, then am I truly all-knowing? Is all this blindness, being temporary — its presence or absence being under my control — nonactual and self-actuated?

"Knowing after" is a kind of looking back, and if what one is looking back upon is no longer present, then the conclusion must be that it never had permanent existence in the first place. The directive for any soul aspiring for Enlightenment would then be to, as the words of the New Testament declare, *"....see swiftly through my folly and madness, invest myself with the shining raiment of wisdom, and place Her on my head as a crown of joy!"*

Following the Eternal Path

Spiritual life and its practice is the singular, most direct, and absolutely certain way of leaving off with the games of our ignorant youth and becoming what we truly and always have been — the All-Abiding *Atman*. "From whence proceeds this pervasive *maya*, with its world-bewitching, soul-intoxicating influence?" is a question best asked only at the early stages of awakening to Truth. *"Go forward,"* as the Great Swan (Sri Ramakrishna) has advised, and following through *"until the Goal of human existence is reached,"* as Swami Vivekananda was so fond of saying, must comprise the following stage, or stages. Otherwise, the soul risks falling into the sleep of ages, continually dreaming heaven, earth, and hell over and over again in a series of births that are unattended by any profound or beneficial kind of "knowing after." — what to speak of Knowing Always.

Certainly, the soul will come to know that it was born, that it knew nothing for a time, that parental upbringing and secularized education erased the blankness of infanthood, etc., but this type of knowledge will not, unfortunately, do away with the unknowing that enforces the illusion of not knowing before. As has been inferred above, certain illumined souls come into the body on earth with a firm grasp upon eternal Wisdom, and even though the *maya* is thick early on, they do all that is required of them by their gurus right away in order to tear away the veil of not-knowing — the Veil of Nescience — and *"be about their Father's business."*

This ability in them becomes a habit, just as the inability of unawakened souls formulates the habit of their tendency for rebirth in ignorance. Recognition of these two kinds of souls, and two kinds of ways of proceeding, is tantamount to overcom-

Six Proofs of Reality In Advaita Vedanta

"Priests, pundits, and other knowers of the Vedas worship various gods. But the Maharishis say that just as the one Ganges manifests herself through many flowing channels, so too does the one Mahashakti express Herself in all deva and devi forms. To come to know this supreme Mahadevi, the best knowers of Truth advise utilizing the seven proofs of the existence of Brahman." — Srimad Devi Bhagavatam

The 6 Proofs of Knowledge
Pramanagatasandeha – Doubt of the 6 Proofs
Pramata – The Measurer, Ego, or Jiva
Pramanachaitanya – Consciousness as Proof
Prameya – The Object of Knowing, Brahman

- Arthapatti — Presumption / Circumstance
- Anupalabdhi — Nonapprehension
- Shabda — Verbal Testimony
- Puranas → Aitijhya — Tradition / Hearsay
- Two Proofs → Sakshi — Witness Consciousness

Perception — Direct, immediate cognition, external and internal, by the ten senses
Presumption — Assumption of a known fact in order to account for an unknown fact
Nonapprehension — Non-perception of a thing based upon the perception of the knower
Analogy — Attainment of knowledge by comparison and similarity
Verbal Testimony — Called apya-vakyas, or agama, it means uttered or written statements
Inference — Called "knowing after," it is a way of gaining knowledge from other knowledge

"Knowledge has come to the soul in two ways, i.e., through the instrumentality of the four inner faculties (antahkarana), and through the five states of consciousness (avasthas) that receive their source material from the five senses. Further, knowing is not a self-contained process, for it receives its initiative and its direction from God. God activates the soul and causes it to know in the same way as the soul activates the five organs of sense and causes them to know." — Saiva-Siddhanta Darshana

> "....where the higher and subtler distinctions like the triputi of knowledge, knower, and the act of knowing disappear and merge, there, the Nondual Reality Shines in Its own halcyon Light of pure, conscious Awareness."

ing the limited ability for only "knowing after," and for generating the truly spiritual quality of all-knowingness, all of the time and beyond time — for time, itself, dictates many of the laws and constrictions around the illusion and acceptance of ignorance (see chart on the facing page).

"I Know, and I Know that I Know!"

The disappearance of ignorance in the human mind is, of course, not as easy as the study of the first proof of Truth makes it seem. To use "knowing after" in conjunction with "suspecting before," or "assuming ahead of time" — like precognitive wisdom in Buddhism — assists the soul immensely in breaking through self-imposed veils and cosmic nescience. For this, the aspirant often takes to an All-knowing Agent that it deems lies beyond the ken of its own currently limited understanding. Since this Agent exists, is Existence Itself, the process, all processes, get truncated, and time begins to play less of a factor in overcoming mental obstacles.

In a song of Mother India, composed by Ramprasad Sen, the poet sings to the Divine Mother of the Universe, *"My very breath and being have become bonded with Your potent mystery, and I experience Your Power as my own inviolate strength. I know, and I know that I know. Liberation from the illusion of not-knowing has been attained only through Thee."*

Herein, within this sweetly complex relationship between God with form and the Formless Reality, lies the precious secret for the consummate devotee, one who courts full remembrance and realization of the innate oneness between nature and Spirit, creature and Creator, God and mankind. The six proofs of Truth, such as verbal testimony, hearsay, and witness consciousness, now come to the fore in the awakened mind of the future luminary, all communicated and exemplified by other intrepid souls who have suspected the ruse pulled upon them by the multi-layered phenomena projected by the cosmic and collective mind. This profound inner movement represents the "timely" death of the limited ability for only "knowing after."

Can Nondual Reality Know Itself?

The scriptures and their seers state, that where the higher and subtler distinctions like the *triputi* of knowledge, knower, and the act of knowing disappear and merge, there, the Nondual Reality Shines in Its own halcyon Light of pure, conscious Awareness. In the Six Proofs of Truth teaching (which this article uses to discuss only the first proof, called *anumana*, "knowing after," - see chart on page 13), the final proof demonstrates this transcendental state. Termed *anupalabdhi*, meaning "nonapprehension," the idea beyond ideas here is that the absence of a person, place, or thing is proof of its existence, as contradictory as that may sound. In the case of name and form in time and space, i.e., *maya*, unreal things appear as real due to its covering power (if one comes to know this fact). In the *anupalabdhi* teaching, nothing is present, leaving the observer with two possible conclusions to draw: first, that nothing exists; second, that Reality is Formless. Of course, both are true, particularly if the former possibility is based upon the fact that appearances like name and form are truly only mere appearances, and have no substance. In the second view, there may be no substance to all and everything, but the knower of Truth comes to know that there is Essence in or behind them.

Essence, with regard to worlds, beings, and objects, appears as substance; *"Brahman appears as the Twenty-Four Cosmic Principles,"* as Sri Ramakrishna has stated. When Essence as substance is not seen or cognized, Its existence is rendered all the more true and real, i.e., the absence of a thing is proof that it once existed. It is much like looking at a vacant lot where a house once stood and concluding that the house existed.

The cogency of this reasoning falls apart if the existence of the perceiver is not affirmed, which explains, in part, why life, memory, families, loved ones, and experiences all disappear when known only by the limited ego, but persist forever in the illumined mind of the Witness, or true Knower. This is the *"nonperception of a thing based upon the perception of the knower."* As Lao Tzu stated, *"The wise one is the one who knows what he does not know."*

If I look up into the nocturnal skies and see a comet coursing by, then look away for a time, then look back the next evening and see the comet no more, its absence is proof of its existence — even if the perceiver does not see it anymore. Similarly, if I look to see God, and succeed in that endeavor, then fall under the influence of *maya's* Curtain of Nescience when I am born again in the body, I still know that God Exists. It is not just speculation, or hope: it is faith; it is Truth. I may have to rely upon the strength of "knowing after" for a time, but that, if taken up consciously and with alacrity, will readily dispense my own inherent wisdom to me in a timely fashion, and thereafter disperse the darkness of ignorance for all time.

Babaji Bob Kindler is the Spiritual Director of the SRV Associations with its main centers in Hawaii, Oregon, and California. A teacher of religion and spirituality and a prolific author, his books include *The Avadhut, Twenty-Four Aspects of Mother Kali, Ten Divine Articles of Sri Durga, Sri Sarada Vijnanagita, Swami Vivekananda Vijnanagita, An Extensive Anthology of Sri Ramakrishna's Stories, A Quintessential Yoga Vasishtha, Reclaiming Kundalini Yoga, and others.* Founder and Artistic Director of Jai Ma Music, he is also an accomplished musician and composer who has produced over twenty-five albums of instrumental and devotional music to date.

The Three Main Factors
In the Attainment of Enlightenment

1 Karma

"Human being; today it is, tomorrow it is not. No one will accompany a person after death. Only action — good and bad — will follow, even after death."
The Holy Mother,
Sri Sarada Devi

2 Practice

"Through spiritual practices, the ties of past karma are cut asunder. But the realization of God cannot be achieved without ecstatic love for Him. Do you know the significance of japa and other spiritual practices? By these, the dominance of the sense-organs is subdued."
Holy Mother, Sri Sarada Devi

Pure Conscious Awareness

3 Time

Kala

Recall life's true purpose
Go on retreat & pilgrimage
Seek out a spiritual path
Find an adept guru
Select an Ishtam / Chosen Ideal
Take final refuge in God
Fulfill all desires in the dharma

Sadhana

Purify the soul via worship
Strengthen body/mind via yoga
Hone the Intellect via study
Memorize the scriptures
Practice japa of the holy mantra
Perceive God with form
Realize the formless Brahman

Karma Vinasha

Awaken to the insidious presence of Maya
Recognize the limitations of name and form in Nature
Perceive the suffering-ridden nature of relative existence
Subdue sense-life by noting the dangers of pleasure and enjoyment
Break free of the cocoon of family life and mundane human convention
Scrutinize the link to one's ancestors and break the chain of rebirth with them
Inspect individual thoughts and habits and connect them to actions in past lifetimes
Meditate with the specific aim to dissolve all mental residue that binds the mind to relativity

"Perhaps one practices japa and austerity in this life. In the next life one intensifies the spiritual mood and in the following advances it further; thus spiritual evolution goes on. The moment that one's karmas come to an end one realizes God. That is one's last birth. This, plus the practice of spiritual discipline, and time, are the factors in the attainment of spiritual knowledge."   Holy Mother, Sri Sarada Devi

◆ *Brother Tadrupa*

WHEN CONSCIOUSNESS IS IN CHARGE

How do we know Consciousness is in charge of our actions? From the conventional point of view, the question might appear absurd. Most people would likely answer that as long as one's mental faculties are in tact i.e., the individual is not insane or have brain damage, then their actions and lives are most likely conscious. *Yoga* Psychology, as utilized in many wisdom *darshanas* (spiritual paths), explored this question to profound and superlative levels far beyond the consideration of the physical brain and nervous system only. In this article, we will inspect teachings put forth by the seers for discriminating between unconscious actions and abidance in Consciousness, as well as how to establish Consciousness in daily spiritual practice.

The Fourfold Mind and the Two Sources of Knowledge

One of Yoga-Vedanta's foundational teachings is that the mind, though insentient, is the mechanism through which the *jivatman* (transmigrating soul) experiences phenomena. Once the mind is purified, the soul realizes Its identity with the *Paramatman* (Supreme Soul). Though *jivatman* and *Paramatman* are essentially one, the mind forgets this. Out of this ignorance comes forth the idea of a separate self. The mind is made of four parts: *manas*, *chitta*, *ahamkara*, and *buddhi*, which can be thought of metaphorically as different tide patterns in an ocean of thought, or different component parts of a single machine. The interplay between the latter two mechanisms holds the key to whether Consciousness is in charge. *Ahamkara* is usually translated as "ego." This, however, does not give a full description, since when we hear the term "ego" we tend to think of someone who has a "big ego" and is puffed up with pride and arrogance. *Ahamkara* is better understood as the "separate I-maker," that is, the portion of the mind responsible for the notion that one is a separate individual. Whenever we think of ourselves as a body-mind aggregate, moving through time and space, this is the workings of the *ahamkara*. Most of our practical day-to-day thinking really pertains to the *ahamkara*, and not to our true Self.

Buddhi is the faculty of reasoning and understanding, the container for intelligence, and the mechanism that makes decisions based on options the mind presents in any given situation. The *buddhi* borrows knowledge from the *Atman* (true Self). A very critical warning, especially for new seekers, is that the *buddhi* can be corrupted or misinformed by the *ahamkara* when the latter is not purified and under control. When this happens, the aspirant bases all their knowledge on the idea of being an individual separate from Divine Consciousness. A scholar who desires validation and glory from their peers is one example. Every new discovery the scholar makes is colored with the notion that "This is my knowledge." The numerous cases of scholars persisting in deluded actions such as plagerism, manipulation of data, and promoting false knowledge for personal gain, are all examples of *ahamkara* corrupting the *buddhi*.

When *buddhi* is misinformed by *ahamkara*, a whole host of problems and obstacles arise for the spiritual seeker, like misunderstanding the spiritual teacher, taking a false *guru* to be an authentic one, attachment to wealth and sensual pleasure, and forgetting that Self-realization is the goal of human existence. Virtually all fears, anxieties, frustrations, and gaps in peace of mind encountered in daily life can be traced back to a misinformed *buddhi*. Take for example a driver who cuts in front of another driver on the road, causing one to yell profanities at the other, causing further discord. Based on this thoughtless action, one driver loses his discernment regarding the knowledge of Divinity as the basis of all happenings. Here, when *ahamkara* usurps the throne of the *Atman* by misinforming the *buddhi*, Consciousness is certainly not in charge. As Sri Krishna explains in sloka 3:27 of the *Bhagavad Gita*, "The gunas of Prakriti perform all action. With buddhi clouded by egotism, man thinks, 'I am the doer.'"

Getting Consciousness in Charge

To get Consciousness in charge of our lives, we have to get proper instruction in what Consciousness really is. How can one with ego-deluded thinking understand, let alone experience, That which is indivisible and transcendent without a proper guide/*guru*? To adapt a story of Sri Ramakrishna, consider a powerful cow that has been tethered to a stake its whole life. It can only move and graze so far because it is thoroughly convinced its activities are limited by the rope and stake. The cow might have the idea of moving to a beautiful mountain it sees far off, but firmly believes the trip to be impossible. To break out of its radius of conditionings, another force, such as a new owner, is required, so that it can move more freely once again.

For one desiring to live in harmony with their true Nature, wisdom scriptures such as the *Upanisads, Yoga Sutras*, and *Bhagavad Gita* are emphatic in their directive to seek out a qualified teacher — one who can give individualized instruction and prescribe spiritual disciplines leading to purification of the mind. This is counterintuitive to the normal thinking processes of the present Technology Age, where one thinks one can attain anything and master it without personal and on-going guidance — like getting fast food at a cheap restaurant. Experiencing the pure atmosphere of Holy Company, especially for extended periods, illustrates to the new seeker what it looks and feels like when Consciousness is in charge. Holy Company provides the tangible metric for Conscious living. It gives the seeker options other than taking refuge in the ego and its desires.

The dynamics of this process is very scientific, which helps support the rationale for on-going spiritual disciplines and frequenting Holy Company repeatedly. In brief, the average mind is colored by a mixture of the three *gunas* (strands) of nature.

These are *tamas* (inertia), *rajas* (restlessness), and *sattva* (balance). It is said that *sattva* reveals the nature of Reality, while *tamas* and *rajas* cover and distort It. The mind of an aspirant is a mixture of all three *gunas*, but generally it cycles between *tamas* and *rajas*. In this condition, one's knowledge proceeds from *ahamkara*, as previously noted. When one enters a sacred spiritual atmosphere that is directed by an illumined *guru*, the very environment radiates with pure *sattva* due to the teacher's transcendental experience of Truth. This *sattva* is unalloyed, meaning unmixed with the lower *gunas*. Attending this atmosphere helps cleanse the *buddhi* of the lower tendencies in the student's mind. Senses and desires get temporarily reduced and subdued, aiding the seeker to better concentrate on subtle truths and train in spiritual disciplines. Devotion to God also increases.

Observing the peaceful and selfless nature of the teacher and his disciples, what it means for Consciousness to be in charge gets gradually imprinted, to varying degrees, in the memory of the seeker. When the student leaves the spiritual center or retreat site they typically experience temporary bliss and clarity of life's purpose. This sometimes is described as having one's torch lit, spiritually speaking. To connect this with the teachings of Sri Ramakrishna, this is the development of ripe ego (*pakvahamkara*). Such an ego is transparent and allows knowledge to proceed from the *Atman*. I can personally remember attending retreats and classes with my teacher early on in spiritual life, and observing over time how my thinking changed dramatically. What seemed important, problematic, or bothersome, simply dissolved in the fire of higher teachings and Holy Company, and the spiritual journey became an increasingly serious priority.

Keeping Consciousness in Charge

Keeping one's torch lit in Consciousness, as previously discussed, while appearing easy when one is surrounded by a group of advanced seekers, turns out to have subtle obstacles. The aspirant needs to develop a vibrant and living spirituality day-to-day until all negative *samskaras* (mental conditionings from desire-based actions) are replaced with positive *samskaras*. To diminish and ultimately eliminate these, one must first carry out and maintain *sadhana* (spiritual disciplines) as instructed by the *guru*. This would likely include cultivating devotion to God, selfless service of the teacher (*mahat seva*), and increasing one's discrimination between the Eternal and non-eternal. In my case, I can recall telling myself as a retreat concluded, "I just have to practice the Four *Yogas* like we did together while on this retreat."

There are many ways in which one's torch can go out, with *ahamkara* getting back in charge. It can be as simple as waking up one day with a conventionally-oriented mindset and priorities. This happens because the mind has passed through *tamas* in going between waking, dreaming, and deep sleep. Also our daily actions, if not carried out with *vairagyam* (detachment), can leave a stain on the mind — like dust getting on a mirror. The mind is to be kept clean and made impervious to these accumulations via a combination of the Four *Yogas*. For example, one might start with a daily practice of thirty minutes of *japa* (recitation of the Lord's name) in combination with devotional exercises such as offering incense and flowers regularly to sacred images of one's Chosen Ideal. Add in the moment-to-moment restraint of mind and senses in action through observing the tenants of *karma yoga*, and we have the essential solution needed to dissolve accumulation of negativities which come as a result of everyday actions. Augmenting this with regular study of nondual scriptures (*jnana yoga*), and a deepening meditation practice (*dhyana yoga*), and the *buddhi* will become a firm and unshakable reflector of the light of the *Atman*. As Sri Krishna instructed in verse 5:20 of the *Bhagavad Gita*, "*Established in Brahman, with buddhi firm and free of delusion, the knower of Brahman rejoices not getting what is pleasant, and grieves not getting what is unpleasant.*" With rightly-oriented perseverance, the seeker will become "*… a lamp unto thyself*," as Lord Buddha advised.

The Destructive Aspect of Consciousness being in Charge

As beings begin to live and think at higher levels of Consciousness, various obstacles and distractions will be revealed. It could be actions, persons, places, and objects that negatively condition our thinking process due to strong attachments or aversions. On a deeper level, it is a false view of Reality (*bhrantidarshana*), either in the past or present, that is the linchpin underlying these challenges. Rather than be dejected over these apparent failures, the devotee must acquire a habit of observing all problems through proper *vichara* (inquiry). Asking the mind questions such as, "What is the motivation being this action?" or, "What is the basis of this mental disturbance?" or, "What does that thought really say about my view of the Universe and myself?" The answers can be sobering at times, but will show where work needs to be done. Some activities may need to be eliminated from our lives.

At a certain point, the seeker will acquire a standard of spiritual integrity which will determine what is acceptable and unacceptable. They will simply and benignly reject anything in their periphery that is unacceptable. As Jesus Christ said, "*We cannot serve both God and Mammon.*" Consciousness being in charge will reveal what is mammon, so that we can get our detachment from it and also utilize our body-mind mechanism towards reaching the Goal. This is the destructive aspect of Truth. Those that embrace it make rapid progress in spiritual life.

Conclusion

Developing a well-rounded spiritual routine and a habit of deep inquiry will help us to a better understand the basic workings of the mind. This will lead to strong conviction about the validity of the techniques and Truths found in revealed scriptures (*vidya shastra*). Engaging in this scientific and hands-on approach to Truth will help establish a sense of abiding peace with oneself, with the Universe, and in our relationship with Reality.

Brother Tadrupa Josh McDaniel is an initiated student of SRV Associations. He has studied with Babaji Bob Kindler for seven years. Tadrupa serves as an advisor to the SRV Board of Directors and assists with various activities such as classes, retreats, and secretarial duties. In his professional life, Tadrupa enjoys serving students as a college math instructor.

◆ SWAMI BRAHMESHANANDA

ahimsa
The Virtue of Nonviolence

"Ahimsa is a goddess who supports all creatures. She is like water for the thirsty, food for the hungry, and medicine for the sick. She conduces to the well-being of all creatures, moving or immobile."
Prashnavykarana

In spite of five millennia of human civilization on earth, fear and violence — the characteristics of sub-human creatures — continue to survive and even flourish as parts of our social and personal lives. We have accepted them as inseparable and unavoidable parts of our culture and civilization. We may not indulge in gross killing of humans or animals in which our aboriginal ancestors indulged, but we have not been able to get over anger, hate, envy, finding fault with others, using harsh words — the subtler aspects of violence. We have evolved newer and more refined means of exploiting others. In spite of the end of the cold war, the arms race is continuing and has become more pervasive. We show greater interest in news of crime and sex, of war and violence, than in others. TV serials and movies depicting war and crime have much greater appeal. All this shows that even after such a long period of civilization, we have remained brutes. Pick up any daily newspaper early in the morning, what do you read? Massacre, murder, rape — violence in so many forms. The newspaper reads like a chronicle of crime. Indeed, we have taken violence for granted as a way of life and something most natural.

But in India, from the very dawn of human civilization, *ahimsà* was extolled as the fundamental human characteristic — *paramo dharmah*, the word *dharma* meaning *vastu-swabhàva* or the basic characteristic of a substance. Just as heat is the *dharma* of fire, so also, our sages said, *ahimsà*, or non-violence is the most important characteristic which differentiates a human being from other animals. Not only this, an attempt was made in ancient India, during the Jain and Buddhistic Movements, as a revolt against the animal sacrifice of Vedic *yajnas*, to build a society with *ahimsà* as the central theme. Emperor Ashoka, on embracing Buddhism, gave *ahimsà* the status of a state-religion. But while the society might have received an ethical lift, it made it weak in the long run. For, although *ahimsà* is the highest ideal, it can truly be practiced only by a rare few in any society at any period of time. Preaching such a high ideal for the whole society — even for those who are not competent to practice it — led to national degradation and a thousand years of slavery. That does not, of course, mean that *ahimsà* is impractical. Indeed, there cannot be a better time to preach and practice *ahimsà* than now. Today, violence has become so pervasive that reiteration of *ahimsà* has become the most urgent need.

Ahimsà is the first and the foremost among the five ethical values called *yama*, the first of the eight limbs of *yoga* as described by Patanjali. Although in the Yoga Sutra, *ahimsà* is prescribed as a spiritual discipline, it is so important that it is considered the very goal of all spiritual endeavour. According to the commentator Vyasa, Truth and other forms of restraints and observances are based on the spirit of non-injury. They, being the means of fulfillment of non-injury, have been recommended in the *shastras* for establishing *ahimsà*.

Thus, one can redefine values like truth and non-covetousness in terms of *ahimsà*. Truth would mean not to harm others directly or indirectly by speaking untruth. Stealing obviously means harming others by taking away something which belongs to them. Hoarding, too, necessarily leads to deprivation of others. *Brahmacharya*, or continence, means not to consider someone else an object of one's enjoyment.

It is not possible to practice non-injury unless selfishness is given up with respect to all external matters. Besides, seeking one's own comfort inevitably involves causing pain to others. Truth, and other forms of restraints and observances, weaken the selfish tendencies of greed and envy, and thereby make *ahimsà* purer.

In the absolute sense, *ahimsà* means the realization of one's solidarity and unity with all creatures, as indicated in the *Isha Upanisad*: *"He who perceives all beings in his own self, and his own self as the self of every being, he does not (by virtue of this perception) hate any one."*

The Jain prophet, Lord Mahavir, has said: *"The being whom you want to kill is none other than you; the being whom you wish to govern and enslave is none other than you. Killing a living being is killing one's own self."*

The direct experience of this highest truth, this transcendental dimension of *ahimsà*, is the goal of all spiritual struggles. Sri Ramakrishna was established in this *pàramàrthika ahimsà*. When due to fatal cancer of the throat he was unable to eat anything himself, he felt that he was eating through the mouths of others. Once, two persons were quarrelling. When one dealt the other a blow, Sri Ramakrishna experienced the pain on his own body. Likewise, at one stage he realized his identity with the grass of the lawn and experienced pain when it was trodden upon. A time came when he could not step upon green grass, since he perceived consciousness in it, and so he walked carefully along dry land.

Vyasa has defined *ahimsà* as, *"....to abstain from injuring any being at any time in any manner."* The Sanskrit word used here for *ahimsà* is *anabhidroha*, i.e. not to have any feeling of enmity, *abhidroha*. According to a similar definition, when evil tendencies like aversion and attachment, hate and envy, do not arise in one's mind, that state is called *ahimsà*. This, then, is the second, the mental or internal, the *àdhyàtmika* dimension of *ahimsà*. And, of course, abstaining from injuring any creature, big or

> "Once, a Sufi saint was passing through a market place. He saw a meat shop and stood at a distance, gazing at the hanging lumps of meat. The shopkeeper noticed him and asked him whether he wanted meat, and even offered it free of cost. The Sufi ascetic declined. At this, the shop-keeper said, half-pleadingly, half-mockingly: 'Although you say you don't need meat, I feel you badly need it. You are emaciated and have no flesh on your body. After all, flesh can be replaced by flesh alone.' What the saint said in reply is significant: 'The amount of flesh sticking to my bones is enough for the worms in the grave.'"

small, moving or immobile, from a worm to a Buddha, by word or deed, is the grossest, or *vyàvahàrika* dimension of *ahimsà*.

There cannot be any controversy that the attainment of the experience of the unity of all existence — the transcendental *ahimsà* — is the goal. According to the *Bhagavad Gita*, that yogi is the best who considers the pleasures and pains of others as his own. Also, there cannot be any objection to the precept that one must try to practice mental *ahimsà* by attempting to get over all ill-feelings and developing goodwill and friendship towards all. But the problem arises when we try to practice *ahimsà* at the physical or external level. For, existence is impossible without killing. Millions of bacteria die as we breathe, eat, and move about. Hundreds of insects die every day, crushed under our feet. The *Srimad Bhagavatam* rightly says, "*Jivo jivasya jivanam: Creatures live on other creatures.*"

A hawk catches a lizard; a lizard eats insects; insects live on plants. Thus life without killing appears impossible. Even in human society, violence appears unavoidable if one has to survive and protect oneself against hostile enemies.

One group of thinkers are of the opinion that to be established in *pàramàrthika ahimsà* is all-important, and if one can attain to it, one need not bother about the empirical or *vyàvahàrika ahimsà*. No sin can accrue to him, who, having realized the oneness of all existence, has become absolutely free from all enmity, even if he were to kill hundreds of people. Sri Krishna seems to advocate this view when he urges Arjuna to fight while being established in spiritual equanimity. Others, however, argue that if one is truly established in *ahimsà*, why should he not practice it externally as well? Nay, one established in *pàramàrthika ahimsà* will not be able to kill, even if he were to try. It will be impossible for such a person to injure any one. He will prefer to give up his own body rather than kill creatures. According to this ideology, all-renouncing sages like Suka are superior to warriors like Rama and Krishna.

Once, a Sufi saint was passing through a market place. He saw a meat shop and stood at a distance, gazing at the hanging lumps of meat. The shopkeeper noticed him and asked him whether he wanted meat, and even offered it free of cost. The Sufi ascetic declined. At this, the shop-keeper said half-pleadingly, half-mockingly: "Although you say you don't need meat, I feel you badly need it. You are emaciated and have no flesh on your body. After all, flesh can be replaced by flesh alone." What the saint said in reply is significant: "The amount of flesh sticking to my bones is enough for the worms in the grave." Indeed, a person established in *ahimsà* would never consider his body superior even to that of a worm, and would never feel inclined to keep it alive at the expense of others.

There was another saint who had a wound infested with maggots. Not only would he not remove the maggots, but would put them back into the wound if any fell out of the wound!

From the above analysis it will be clear that there are three levels, or grades, of *ahimsà*: *pàramàrthika*, or transcendental; *àdhyàtmika* or mental; and *vyàvahàrika* or practical. Of these, the *pàramàrthika* is the goal, while the other two are the means. It is obvious that mental *ahimsà* is superior to mere gross physical practice of *ahimsà*, so every attempt must be made to become as non-violent in our thoughts and feelings as possible.

Ahimsà is not a single or isolated virtue. It is a conglomeration of numerous values. Peace, love, compassion, fearlessness, protection, goodwill, cheerfulness, etc., are all various aspects of this one virtue, *ahimsà*. Love, intimacy, sacrifice, equanimity, same-sightedness, and compassion are the very basis of *ahimsà*, and must be carefully cultivated.

Anyone who wishes to practise *ahimsà* must, at the very outset, deeply impress upon his mind the absolute necessity of *ahimsà*, and its superiority over other values. "*Ahimsà is the very basis of harmonious and peaceful living. Every creature has a right to live peacefully. Less killing is better living.*" Such ideas must be repeatedly impressed upon one's mind.

A person who voluntarily embraces a spiritual life resolves to impart fearlessness to all creatures. If such a spiritual aspirant is compelled to inflict physical, verbal, or mental pain or injury on any creature, he must feel repentant and think, "Fie on me that after granting freedom from fear to creatures I am breaking my resolve by inflicting pain on them. Oh, I am not fully established in *ahimsà*." Such a self-reproach is extremely useful in strengthening the feeling and mood of *ahimsà*. One must never approve of violence in any form. Swami Vivekananda has said, "*There is no such thing as righteous anger or justifiable killing.*"

Patanjali has recommended the practice of thinking opposite thoughts, *prati-paksha bhàvanam*, when perverse thoughts and impulses related to violence prompt us to act against *ahimsà*. Vyasa gives an illustration of this while commenting upon the pertinent Yoga Sutra:

"*These actions like killing etc., lead to endless consequent suffering and ignorance. The killer first reduces the power of the victim by tying him up; then inflicts pain by weapons, and finally kills. As a consequence of these, the injurer loses the vigour of his body, mind, and senses. On account of causing pain he suffers in infernal regions and is reborn as an animal or an evil spirit; and for killing, either he suffers from fatal illness or goes on suffering continuously."*

We generally feel envious when we find those people happy by whom our self-interest might be jeopardized, or who are our competitors. Similarly, a cruel delight is felt when we find an enemy becoming unhappy or in distress. The reputation of pious persons of a different denomination or group often excites jealousy and displeasure. We are prone to find fault with such people even though there may be none. Finally, we feel anger or become cruel towards people who commit sin. Such reactions of envy, cruel delight, and malevolence or anger, are not conducive to the practice of *ahimsà*. Hence, Patanjali recommends that feelings of amity, compassion, goodwill, and indifference must be cultivated towards the happy, miserable, virtuous, and sinful respectively.

One may incorporate such short prayers conveying this idea in one's daily devotional practice: "May I be friendly towards all; delight in seeing the meritorious; be compassionate towards the sufferers, and remain indifferent towards those with a contrary temperament."

Finding fault with others, using harsh, abusive language, criticizing people, trying to go ahead of others in any sphere of life by pushing them from behind, or competing with them — these are all subtle modes of violence. They have become an inseparable part of our existence. These must first be recognized and accepted as undesirable and contrary to the ideal of *ahimsà*. Then only shall we be able to get over them.

Since all creatures are, in the absolute sense, one, and since the goal of *ahimsà* is to intuitively realize one's solidarity with all creation, to meditate constantly on this truth and to direct and attune one's thoughts and actions according to this highest truth, is the most direct and immediate practice of *ahimsà*. Let us constantly remind ourselves that the worm crawling on the path, the cat, the dog, the beggar, the thief, the saint and the sinner — all are our own self. This feeling, at the psychological level, flowers into love in its truest sense.

Mahatma Gandhi, too, equates *ahimsà* with love. There could be no better exemplar of this than the Holy Mother, who could say that she was the mother of all, even of insects and moths. Her central message, *"Do not find fault with others. None is a stranger, my child. All are your own. Learn to make the whole world your own,"* is the most important and practical instruction for *ahimsà*. Although Swami Vivekananda's cardinal message centers round the concept of *mukti*, or freedom, he does not underrate *ahimsà*: *"If your freedom hurts others, you are not free there. You must not hurt others."*

As one strengthens one's resolve to live as non-violently as possible by the above mentioned means, one must also try to practice *ahimsà* at the empirical level. First of all, one must give up, once and for all, conscious, deliberate, planned, or willed acts of injuring others, by word or by deed. Felling trees, killing of insects in agriculture or for procuring one's livelihood, are generally accepted modes of *himsà*, violence. Violence involved in self-defense, and in following one's profession also cannot be altogether avoided. However, one must try to reduce them to a minimum. This has become all the more urgent today when ecological imbalance caused by extravagant living styles of human beings is assuming threatening proportions. One must be very careful to see that no harmless creature, which can be saved with a little carefulness, is hurt unnecessarily.

Then there are grades of violence. The vileness of one's injurious acts varies with the intensity of the evil intention. Killing a man and cutting grass do not involve the same amount of cruelty. Again, hurting a man with rude words is not the same as killing him. Killing an assailant enemy is not considered *himsà* or evil in common parlance.

These gradations in the practice of *ahimsà* may be valid for an ordinary person, but yogis try to practice *ahimsà* in its totality, as a supreme vow, *mahàvrata*. First of all, they refrain from doing even the least harm to human beings, even to an offender or an armed attacker. Next, they inflict as little injury to sub-human creatures as possible. They would, for example, frighten away a snake rather than kill it. Then, they try to practice harmlessness towards the vegetable kingdom by not hurting even plants. They neither inflict injury, nor cause it to be inflicted by others, nor approve of it.

It cannot be over-emphasized that the practice of values like truthfulness, non-possessiveness, non-stealing, etc., are indispensable for excellence in *ahimsà*, for, as has already been pointed out, falsehood, hoarding, and stealing are, in fact, various facets of *himsà*, or violence. A simple, pure, peaceful life, free from pretensions, is essential for *ahimsà*. This has become all the more important today when life has become so complicated and we have become so dependent on others. Every increase in one's comfort and luxury puts a corresponding stress on others.

Charity, service, and helping others in various ways are the positive facets of *ahimsà*, and some people emphasize them more than abstaining from injuring others. The two are interrelated. One cannot be a non-violent person if one injures some to help others. The negative, abstaining aspect of *ahimsà* is equally important.

Like all other moral values, the practice of *ahimsà*, too, has problems and difficulties, and even exceptions. A poor man, who has to struggle hard for his and his family's existence may have *ahimsà* as the ultimate goal, but cannot accept it as the immediate means. Likewise, a nation, constantly threatened by external enemies, cannot resort to unconditional *ahimsà*. *Ahimsà* would make a weak person weaker, for *ahimsà* and forgiveness glorify only the strong and the brave.

The second problem is that, in due course, the means themselves become the ends. The method is emphasized so much that the goal is totally forgotten. This holds true for *ahimsà* also. Fanatics spend all their time and attention in saving insects and feeding birds and ants, and feel guilty if an insect is killed, and yet they do not try to get over envy, hate, and anger. They forget that the goal of the practice of *ahimsà* is to realize that one's Soul is the Soul of all, and all are in one's own Self.

It is easy to understand and put into practice the grosser, physical aspect of any spiritual value. Besides, it is obvious, and also gains recognition from the people around. To abstain from external killing is easy, but it is extremely difficult to totally get rid of envy, anger, and hatred. Hence *ahimsà*, in the course of time, gets reduced to heartless vegetarianism and non-killing of tiny creatures, its subtler aspect being totally forgotten.

Whatever might be the problems and difficulties, every one must try to practice *ahimsà* to the best of his ability and according to the station in life he or she is placed in. To the extent an individual truly practices *ahimsà*, and to the extent *ahimsà* is practiced in a society, to that extent can that individual or society be considered civilized. *Ahimsà* is then the standard, the yardstick, by which the evolution of a society or an individual can be measured.

(This article has been reprinted with the permission of Vedanta Keshari)

A former editor of the Vedanta Keshari, and previously of the Ramakrishna Mission Home of Service, Swami Brameshananda is a senior monk of the Ramakrishna Order and until recently was the Secretary of the Ramakrishna Mission Ashram in Chandigarh, India. Over the years his writings in Hindi and English have appeared in several journals, including Prabuddha Bharata, Vedanta Keshari, and Nectar of Nondual Truth. He specializes in themes related to Jainism. He is now retired and is living in Varanasi.

Ahimsa in the Mahabharata

One should never do that to another which one regards as injurious to one's self. This, in brief, is the rule of dharma. Yielding to desire and acting differently, one becomes guilty of adharma.

Those high-souled persons who desire beauty, faultlessness of limbs, long life, understanding, mental and physical strength and memory, should abstain from all acts of injury.

*Ahimsa is the highest dharma.
Ahimsa is the best tapas.
Ahimsa is the greatest gift.
Ahimsa is the highest self-control.
Ahimsa is the highest sacrifice.
Ahimsa is the highest power.
Ahimsa is the highest friend.
Ahimsa is the highest truth.
Ahimsa is the highest teaching.*

"All breathing, existing, living, sentient creatures should not be slain, nor treated with violence, nor abused, nor tormented, nor driven away. Kill not, cause no pain. Nonviolence is the greatest religion." —Mahavir

Wisdom Facets From the Gem of Truth

Sri Ramakrishna

Holy Mother, Sri Sarada Devi

"I am Too Busy to Do That!"

"A devotee asked Ramakrishna: "Can't we realize God without complete renunciation?" He said: "Of course you can! Why should you renounce everything? You are all right as you are, following the middle path – like molasses partly solid and partly liquid. I tell you the truth: there is nothing wrong with your being in the world. But you must direct your mind toward God; otherwise you will not succeed. Do your duty with one hand and with the other hold to God. After the duty is over you will hold to God with both hands. You should say to Him: 'O God, make my worldly duties fewer and fewer; otherwise, O Lord, I find that I forget Thee when I am involved in too many activities. I think am doing unselfish work, but it turns out to be selfish.' It is not good to become involved in many activities."

(Gospel of Sri Ramakrishna)

Called by Whatever Name.....

"According to the Shaktas, a perfected soul is called a kaul. In the Vedanta he is called a paramahamsa. The Vaishnavas call him a sai. There is none greater. Hindus call him nir, and Muslims call him pir. With Ultimate Reality, the sai calls It Alekh, the Incomprehensible. In the Vedas It is called Brahman. They say of the individual soul that it comes and departs, that is to say, that it comes from the unmanifest and then merges back into It."

(Sri Sri Ramakrishna Kathamrita)

Utterly Sound Advice

"As cows eat their fill of fodder mixed with oil-cake and water, then sit and happily chew the cud, likewise, after visiting temples and holy places, one should sit in a secluded spot to ruminate and become absorbed in the godly thoughts that arose in the mind there. After visiting sacred places one should not immediately put one's mind on worldly things and drive holy thoughts away. If that happens, those godly thoughts cannot leave permanent impressions on the mind."

(Gospel of Sri Ramakrishna)

Food Is Brahman

"My child, your body is also my body; I suffer if you do not keep good health. Eating food that has not been offered is equivalent to eating sin. The place and manner in which it is prepared is also important. So first, offer to God whatever you eat. One must not eat unoffered food. As your food is, so will be your blood. From pure food you will get pure blood, pure mind and strength. Pure mind begets Prema, ecstatic Love."

(Sri Sarada Vijnanagita)

Awakening by Stages

"About realization and spiritual attainment, just think that you are fast asleep on a cot in this room. At night, in your sleep state, you are carried on your cot to a different room. What will you feel the moment you wake up and open your eyes? You will feel that you are in the same place as you were before. But a little later, when you finally shake off your drowsiness, you will see that you have, in fact, come to a totally different place. At that time you will think, 'Where was I, and where have I arrived now?'"

(The Compassionate Mother)

Grace is Yours: Now Work hard to Realize It

"You need not do anything. Whatever is needed, I will do. All that I needed to do, I have done for you at the time of your initiation. But if you want immediate peace, you must take recourse to spiritual disciplines; otherwise, you will get the benefits only after death."

(The Compassionate Mother)

The Best Bargain in the Three Worlds!

"Through the mantra, spiritual energy is transmitted — the guru's energy goes to the disciple, and the disciple's sins come over to the guru. That is why imparting mantras and taking over sins, the body becomes afflicted with so many diseases. That is why Rakhal tells me, 'Mother, I suffer from fever when I impart the mantra."

(The Compassionate Mother)

Wisdom Facets From the Gem of Truth

Swami Vivekananda   Disciples & Devotees of Sri Ramakrishna

Work as Worship, Seva as Service

"After realization, what is ordinarily called work does not persist. It changes its character. The work which the jnani does only conduces to the well-being of the world. Whatever a man of realization says or does contributes to the welfare of all."

(Talks with Swami Vivekananda)

Only Renunciation is Fearless

"Throw away those bhakti texts that teach that renunciation kills the feelings that make for tenderness. Without burning renunciation, dispassion for sense objects, and turning away from wealth and lust as from filthy abominations, never can one attain to salvation even in hundreds of Brahma's cycles. Repeating the names of the Lord, meditation, worship, offering libations into sacred fire, penance — all of these are for bringing forth renunciation. One who has not gained renunciation, know his efforts to be like unto those of a man who is pulling at the oars all night while the boat remains at anchor."

(Talks with Swami Vivekananda)

The Epiphany of the First Noble Truth

"This world is and is not, manifold yet one. I shall unravel its mystery, and I shall know whether grief be there or anything else. I do not flee from it as from a bugbear. I will know all about it. As to the infinite pain that attends its search, I am embracing it in its fullest measure."

(Swami Vivekananda Vijnanagita)

New Lights for Old

"We now have a new India, with its new God, new religion, and new Vedas. When, O Lord, shall our land be free from this eternal dwelling upon the past? He who has no faith in Him, and no reverence for the Mother, will be a downright loser. I tell you plainly, Sri Ramakrishna has given us refuge. What more do you want?"

(Swami Vivekananda Vijnanagita)

Masseuse of the Gods....

"One day while meditating at home I had a vision of the omnipresent eyes of God. Those open eyes were all-pervading, like the limitless sky. Thus everyday in the morning and before going to sleep I would be absorbed in deep meditation and I would see the divine forms of various gods and goddesses, and I used to go to Dakshineswar and describe these to Paramahamsadeva. Sometimes he would allow me to rub His feet...."

(Swami Abhedananda, My Life-Story)

Time for the Truth

"It does not follow that Vedanta is dead or asleep among us. Some of us regard these breathing periods as the most valuable influence of all, in extending the sphere of conviction. The thoughts that Vedantic teaching brings, to a mind hearing it for the first time, are too vast and too new in kind for speedy assimilation. There must be rest and solitude, and fate has ordained that instead of our going away into the wilderness to find these, our interpreters shall go away from us and leave us to fight with our ignorance alone."

(Sister Nivedita, in Atmaprana)

Covering All Spiritual Bases

"It is good to be active, but action depends on several factors. First, your health must be good. You should also be able to get along with your co-workers. But suppose you injure one of your limbs. Then it would be difficult for you to work. There you should cultivate the habit of study and reading. But even that might not be enough. Suppose you become blind? Therefore, it is good that you also practice meditation so that if you cannot read or work, at least you can meditate on God."

(Swami Saradananda, Glimpses of a Great Soul)

SCRIPTURAL SAYINGS
of the World's Religious Traditions

"Having slain mother, father, two kings of the Brahmin caste, and a tiger as the fifth, that accomplished one who thus destroys the five hindrances of lust, ill will, torpor, restlessness, and doubt, goes along his peaceful way, unperturbed."

"Our Lord and Saviour did not arrange the manner of his own death lest He should seem to be afraid of some other. He accepted and bore upon the cross a death inflicted by others, his special enemies, a death which to them was supremely terrible and by no means to be faced; and He did this in order that by destroying even this death, He might Himself be believed to be the Life, and the power of death be finally annulled. A marvelous and mighty paradox has thus occurred, for the death which they thought to inflict on him as dishonor and disgrace has become the glorious monument to death's defeat."

"After mystic fusion with The Beloved, the vagabond of Love, friend of all souls, wanders through the grand prayer hall of creation, the sacred temple of divine manifestation, taking delight solely in the invocation of 'Allah.' His reign is timeless, removed from the fleeting quality of life. The eyes of his intuition have been clarified by perceiving all religions as spokes within one wheel of revelation."

"Perceiving the suffering of this finite world, one should turn to the Atman, the Unborn, who is Infinite. When mind enters Atman its variances are seen as unreal, and Peace descends. Atman is like intense concentration without end, but free of conceptualization. Atman has neither destruction nor origination – bondage nor salvation nor emancipation. This is the highest Truth! In its dynamic phase It diversifies entities. Those few who recognize Atman's envisionings perceive Its beauty everywhere. For them, no difference between Jiva and Atman exists whatsoever. Thus, illumined seers declare: Nonduality alone is auspicious!"

"It is indeed surprising that a man, inspite of his belief in the Fires of Hell, is still able to laugh, and inspite of his belief in suffering he is able to be happy. Inspite of believing in the Reckoning he commits evil deeds. Inspite of believing in bliss he still grieves. Inspite of observing the world with its changes he feels contented with it. Inspite of believing in morality and justice, he still refrains from righteous deeds. Does he not know that the dust returns to the ground it came from, and the spirit returns to God who gave it?"

"Embracing Tao, you become embraced. Supple, breathing gently, you become reborn. Clearing your vision, you become clear. Nurturing your beloved, you become impartial. Opening your heart, you become accepted. Accepting the World, you embrace Tao. Bearing and nurturing, creating but not owning, giving without demanding, controlling without authority – This is Love."

Qi
Health & Immortality in Daoist Self-Cultivation

Spiritual practice often focuses on mind related practices. The body has its significance too. Generally, having a healthy and ill-free body not only ensures smooth spiritual progress but a healthy body often also primarily prepares for further higher stages of spiritual development. Human body condition and diet influence mind (mind and its relation with five senses, cognition, emotions, thoughts, and intellect) and vice versa, the mental state of mind have influence over the body. Both body (first body, second mind) and mind should be given attention in spiritual practice in my opinion. If the body is not first taken care of, then mind training becomes difficult.

Also, a healthy physical body, in the view of Daoist medicine and traditional Chinese medicine, is indispensable for advanced stages of seated meditation. The body without ailments prevents later unwanted difficulties during the meditation.

Worldly people are led by their body and bodily desires. However, a saint directs his body from his mind, and is always in a state of equilibrium of mind. For most people and spiritual novices, entering a spiritual path often begins with the gross aspect of the body. They then proceed from the gross to the subtle element of Qi (aka chi) 氣 often comparable to and known as *prana* in Indian *Yogic* traditions. Whether or not words such as 'Qi' 氣 and "*prana*" are pointing toward the exact same substance in real life is irrelevant here. To find a univocal definition for Qi is not my concern. This article only intends to give insight into the former type of "energy."

Body, Qi 氣, and mind are interrelated. Many Chinese Mountain Wudang Daoist-originated practices or bodily health exercises exist, where mind also get "cleansed" or "cleared" through manipulation of the body. For the highest Daoist spiritual attainment, namely Daoist immortality, a healthy body, and mind are preparatory. Quanzhen Daoists view different life-nurturing methods as crucial prerequisites for spiritual enlightenment and Immortal-hood. Daoist physical exercises are also able to open bodily energetic channels or meridians – for example, "eight pieces of brocade" or Ba Duan Jin 八段錦 and "eight pieces of diamond practice" or Ba Bu Jin Gang Gong 八部金剛功. So, the Daoist or Chinese concept of Qi is vast and complex. This article serves as an introduction and short discourse mainly on Qi 氣, Daoist immortality, and self-cultivation – inner transformation from gross to subtle, subtle to the spirit, then spirit to Daoist emptiness and at last primordial union with the Dao.

Health and Inner Cultivation

Daoist self-cultivation and traditional Chinese Medicine are interrelated. The Chinese have a characteristic system of ways of keeping the human body healthy. A variety of healing methods are known today which ultimately are derived from very ancient manuscripts, medical textbooks, and self-cultivation manuals. Healing methods in Daoism vary from acupuncture, herbs, and massages to Fengshui geomancy/cosmology, seasonal diets, Daoyin gymnastics, Daoist meditation, to Qigong and Taijiquan. These healing methods are more or less all centered on the concept of Qi 氣. In the Chinese mind Qi is something which is all around us, tangible or intangible to the senses. It plays an important role in self-cultivation of the human being in the Daoist context. To obtain a clear understanding of what Qi actually is, I think, one should have experiential knowledge through practice or feeling the manifestation of Qi through a Actual Qi experience, basic theoretic knowledge on the subject, is indispensable.

The main Daoist view of self-cultivation, especially in neidan 內丹 or inner alchemy, is transforming the gross to the subtle, converting subtle to spirit or shen 神, then finally reverting shen into xu 虛 or Daoist notion of emptiness, returning to the Dao 道. In other words, there are three stages of development (three Daoist treasures), namely jing Qi, shen 精氣神; translated as nutritive essence (originally in the human body, such as semen, blood, ovaries, and the food we consume), Qi (internal energy, pneuma), and shen 神, meaning spirit/supernatural being (internal soul or optimum state of internal forces). These are also known as the "way of jindan" 金丹道 or the "Way of Golden Elixir."

Among the numerous Daoist schools which practices vary in time and place throughout Chinese history, most Daoist schools have *neidan* as an important practice. The foundation for most forms and lineages of Daoist alchemy is the *Cantong qi* 參同契 or *Seal of the Unity of the Three*, attributed to Wei Boyang 魏伯陽 from 2nd century CE. This work lays down the most complete exposition of the *neidan* principles and their application.

In this article, the main concern is with Chinese Wudang mountain Complete Perfection Quanzhen school of Daoism. This school is characterized not only by its focus on *neidan*, but also by the integration of Confucian and Chinese Buddhist ideas, borrowing elements from Chinese Chan Buddhism 禪宗. *The Heart Sutra, Diamond Sutra, Heroic Progress Sutra,* and *Perfection of Wisdom Sutra*. Also, early Chinese Buddhist schools like *Tiantai* 天台 and *Chan* 禪 influenced Daoist Neidan considerably, but this subject will not be explored here. Likewise, esoteric Buddhist hand *mudra's* made their way into the Quanzhen sect through Zhenyan Buddhism 真言宗, more widely known under the Japanese name of Shingon Buddhism. This syncretic idea is known as the Three Teachings, or *Sanjiao* 三教 (Confucianism, Daoism and Buddhism). The outlook of the Quanzhen masters is that the Three Teachings are ultimately the same religion; different paths and expressions of the ultimate and only reality, the Dao. For further reading on Quanzhen Daoist branch for a more complete view of Daoism, see *The Encyclopedia of Taoism vol. I and vol. II*, edited by Fabrizio Pregadio. Even though the Quanzhen sect emphasizes the Three Teachings, at the core of its doctrines the emphasis is still on *Neidan* to attain Immortal-hood and ascend to Heaven.

> *"'Human life is the accumulation of Qi; death is its dispersal.'* In the Daoist conception, Qi is the vital energy that makes life possible for human beings. One of the definitions for Qi is: the basic substance in nature or the material energy of the universe. Literally, Qi means "air," "cloud," "breath," or "vapor." Defining Qi only in this way is, however, not quite the whole picture."

Defining Qi

Two written texts from the Daoist encyclopedia Yunji Qiqian 雲笈七籤 (Seven Slips from a Cloudy Satchel), found in the Daoist Canon (DZ 1032, fasc. 677-702), are prominent in providing knowledge about avoiding illness and attaining longevity. Both texts cover information about Qi 氣 related to nourishing life. The first one is the Fu Qi jingyi lun 服氣精義論 (Discourse on the Essential Meaning of Absorption of Qi) in chapter 57, written by Sima Chengzhen 司馬承禎 (647-735) who had the title of the twelfth patriarch of the Shangqing or Highest Clarity school of Daoism. The second one is the Sheyang zhenzhong fang 攝養枕中論 (Pillowbook of Methods for Nourishing Life) in chapter 33, ascribed to Sun Simiao 孫思邈 (581?-682) was an outstanding Daoist, alchemist, and physician throughout his life: *"Human life is the accumulation of Qi; death is its dispersal."* In the Daoist conception, Qi is the vital energy that makes life possible. One of the definitions for Qi is: the basic substance in nature or the material energy of the universe. Literally, Qi means "air", "cloud", "breath", or "vapor." Defining Qi this way is only part the picture.

The Chinese character for Qi can be separated into two parts, each with a different meaning. The first part has the meaning of a person eating and the second part means grain in a pot. However, Qi is not merely derived from food intake. Basically, it is the essential life force within and without all living phenomena. On the postnatal plane Qi comes in different modes and many different levels of subtlety, yet from the Daoist medicine and Traditional Chinese Medicine point of view, of importance is yuanqi 元氣 or Original Qi/Original pneuma. From Original Qi are derived two types of Qi. The first type is *xiantian Qi* 先天氣 prenatal Qi or pre-heaven/pre-celestial Qi. The second type is *houtian Qi* 後天氣, postnatal Qi, or post-heaven/post-celestial Qi. Prenatal Qi functions as a connection between people and the universe, whereas postnatal Qi functions in supporting the human body in its everyday renewal and survival. Postnatal Qi is derived from fresh air inhalation, pure food consumption at the right season and time of day, sunlight absorption (preferably watching sunrise and sunset), in human interaction, but also sexual hygiene and emotional aspects.

The circulation of Original Qi inside the body, where prenatal Qi and postnatal Qi are considered as one, not only maintains the material body but also supports the mental and spiritual processes of the human. Feelings are caused by material changes and material changes are caused by feelings. In other words, the expression of feeling is related to the well-being of a person and vice versa. Certain emotions can affect Qi functions as well. According to early classics, excessive and undisciplined emotion causes disease. For example in a tractate on the causes of pain in the Basic Questions of the Inner Canon of the Yellow Lord, it states: *"I know that all medical disorders arise from Qi. Anger (nu 怒) makes the Qi rise; joy (xi 喜) relaxes it; sorrow (bei 悲) dissipates it; fear (kong 恐) makes it go down; cold contracts it; heat makes it leak out; fright (jing 驚) makes its motion chaotic; exhaustion consumes it; worry (si 思) congeals it."* The emotion expressed by a person causes a physical change in the body. The circulation of Qi will deviate from its natural flow, and when a certain emotion is excessive could it lead to ailments. Therefore, emotional balance and a tranquil mind also have a positive effect on bodily health.

For human beings to stay alive, having both types of Qi is necessary. The two types of Qi have constant interaction with each other. They can be imagined as an earth globe with its core inside and the periphery around it. At the core, there exists prenatal Qi and the postnatal Qi surrounds the core at the periphery. When the amount of postnatal Qi in the body is abundant, it also directly complements the prenatal Qi inside the body. It results in the prenatal Qi becoming complete. This complete prenatal Qi can be found prenatally in fetuses, since fetuses are totally dependent on their mother's nourishment and excluded from the outside world. So they have no direct Qi-interaction between postnatal Qi and their prenatal Qi. In other words, fetuses do not possess postnatal Qi, and only have complete prenatal Qi.

There seems to be a clear connection between the two types of Qi; the amount of postnatal Qi affects the amount of prenatal Qi in a person. When the amount of postnatal Qi is abundant, then the person reaches complete prenatal Qi. This is beneficial for the well-being of a person. What happens if the amount of postnatal Qi is deficient? Under such circumstances it means that the less postnatal Qi there is, the less prenatal Qi there is inside the body. This may result in emotional problems, fatigue or illness of body (bodily suffering), and negativity invading body and mind from outside body. However, to lose postnatal Qi and thereby prenatal Qi is a slow process. Shallow breathing, improper nutrition, emotional outbursts, sensory overloads, intellectual tensions, and excessive sexual ejaculations of the male are some of the main causes of losing prenatal Qi.

Moreover, in some cases when a person has lost a considerable amount of prenatal Qi and is unable to replenish (bu kui補虧) it to balance, then healing is crucial.

Healing methods vary from acupuncture, massages, diets, herbs, and gymnastics, to breathing methods and conscious lifestyle changes. These healing methods, more or less, share a common purpose, which is to stimulate the prenatal Qi of patients back to a well-balanced amount so that their health will be in good condition. Looking at this concept we may wonder whether it is possible for healthy people who are not in the situation of prenatal Qi-deficiency and not ill at all, to also raise their amount of prenatal Qi through some of these healing methods? This is possible in the Daoist context, but obviously, the purpose of the latter group of people is different. They aim to raise their healthy amount of prenatal Qi backward to full and complete prenatal Qi, a reversal to a state of being unborn; chun yang xiantian zhi Qi 純陽先天之氣, translated as pure Yang Qi of pre-heaven. A healthy body is fundamentally a stepping stone for further Daoist spiritual self-cultivation.

Daoist Goal of Immortality

To regain complete prenatal Qi in Daoist self-cultivation is a way of dealing with the afterlife, and here lies the primary goal – to attain spiritual immortality. However, prior to this, Daoists were, in the beginning, fascinated by the idea of the possibility of achieving bodily immortality. They were especially captivated by the attributes of the youthful physique. So they believed in inventions of certain techniques to bring aging to a halt, or even return the physical body similar to that of a young healthy person. Later this idea shifted towards belief in that the inherent factors of senescence lies in the Three Worms (sanchong三蟲) or the Three Cadavers (sanshi三尸). Their aspiration was to eject these from the body to become spiritual/immortal, called immortal/god xian 仙, and to live on in an eternal postnatal kind of paradise (heaven) with a youthful body. To attain this, special rites had to be prepared before death and apart from this, and more importantly, was putting a lifelong effort into practice.

Practitioners of Daoist self-cultivation/internal cultivation aiming at immortality should have complete prenatal Qi before they refine it into subtler forms. Having finer Qi does not directly lead to spiritual immortality. Practitioners must first undergo intensive meditation, special diet, and longevity techniques. Only then will the finer Qi turn into pure spirit, or shen神.

Daoist exercises have a connection to the subtle energy realm in the nature of human beings. The subtle energy realm or subtle energy body shows a spiritual structure, and is built out of energy centers called dantian 丹田, and meridians (pathways of energy). Qi and three dantian (lower one below the navel, middle one at heart, higher one at third eye above eyebrows) can be developed and meridians can be activated and opened through Daoist exercises that are connected with certain body postures, movement, breathing, relaxation, and mental concentration. Qi can be accumulated in the lower dantian 丹田, which is about three inches below the navel.

The word "spiritual" in "spiritual immortality" in the Daoist context refers to this pure spirit, or shen. The second word, "immortality," stands for the transition of the human body into another dimension of Qi-operation, and thereby exceeding the natural order of the human body. In other words, the physical body will decay, but that does not prevent the spirit-body from living on as a supernatural being in the godly Daoist heaven realm of bliss. Daoist spiritual immortality is difficult to achieve because of the required discipline and long time of study and mastery. In addition, the practice of moving postnatal Qi intentionally could harm health, and thus should be done with great caution and always under supervision. Special diets should be done with care, and only under the guidance of an experienced teacher. When aiming for health and longevity, for example, deep abdominal breathing is advisable. Here the diaphragm expands on inhalation. However, when aiming for spiritual immortality, reversed breathing is preferable. Contrary to deep abdominal breathing, the diaphragm then expands on exhalation in reversed breathing. The latter type of breathing is an advanced level of breathing, and should only be done at a higher stage and under supervision. Otherwise, it could cause complications from dizziness to disorientation, or worse. So practicing Daoist spiritual cultivation and immortality should be done with caution. Dietary techniques and respiratory techniques are just two out of six practices to become a spiritual immortal. The other four are heliotherapeutic techniques, gymnastic techniques, sexual hygiene (interestingly, most Quanzhen Daoists have abandoned "bedroom" and deity visualization practices. They believe the latter is a form of make-believe), and alchemical and pharmaceutical techniques.

Flow of Qi

To presume that self-cultivation is principally about storing up as huge a quantity of prenatal Qi as possible, is a misinterpretation. The well-being of a person is rather about having just the right amount of prenatal Qi. However, a huge amount of prenatal Qi does result in a better metabolic function of the body. As already observed, every person has a well-balanced amount of Qi from birth. The quantity of prenatal Qi is not only important for health. Moreover, the amount of Qi must be in harmony and especially have a smooth unobstructed flow in energy channels.

Smooth Qi-flow is an integral part of what leads to good health. But the opposite of this may also occur. Take for example a dam in a waterway system. The dam acts as an obstruction in the waterway system, and a reverse force affects the smoothly flowing water. This obstruction creates an imbalance into the whole waterway system and ultimately brings problems like drought or flood. This example of obstruction in the waterway system can also be envisioned inside the body. Similar to the water flow is the flow of Qi. If Qi does not flow smoothly then it can give rise to ailments. So, part of what will make people healthy is a smooth Qi-flow running in a harmonious manner.

This state of Qi-flow could be called zhengqi 正氣. It means "Proper Qi" or "upright Qi" in English. Ideally, the Qi flows freely in the body without any obstructions, so the body is in balance and harmony. The opposite of this is called xieqi 邪氣. This

> "The word 'spiritual' in 'spiritual immortality' in the Daoist context refers to this pure spirit, or shen. The second word, "immortality," stands for the transition of the human body into another dimension of Qi-operation, and thereby exceeding the natural order of the human body. In other words, the physical body will decay, but that does not prevent the spirit-body from living on as a supernatural being in godly Daoist heaven realm of bliss. Daoist spiritual immortality is difficult to achieve because of the required discipline and long time of study and mastery."

is also translated as "deviant Qi," "pathogenic Qi," "heteropathic Qi," or "evil Qi". *Xieqi* negatively affects the body's natural adaptation to changes outside the body. Explained in a different manner, whereas *zhengqi* supports the body in its everyday renewal, and to function in society with vigor and longevity, *xieqi* does the contrary. In the state of xieqi, the harmonious, steady, strong and smooth Qi-flow is disrupted and is confused. In other words, it does not follow the natural order of Qi-flow. The transformation to this state, however, is slow, but when *xieqi* becomes dominant in the body it affects the health negatively and causes exhaustion of the body's resources.

For detachment of the inside rhythm of Qi-flow from the outside natural rhythm, there are several facets. First, the speed or pace of Qi-flow in the body moves either too fast or too slow. Second, the amount of prenatal Qi is excessive or depleted. Third, rushes or blockages appear in the Qi-flow. In summary, illness is derived from anything which negatively influences the right amount and the natural flow of Qi. Furthermore, the term "excessive" in "excessive Qi" must not be confused with the same interpretation as "abundant." That is, excessive Qi does not refer to the amount of Qi inside the body that has risen into a surplus, nor does it mean new prenatal Qi is created. Excessive Qi is developed by external factors, meaning outside the body, like the body has been exposed to too much heat or cold. Other causes than extreme temperatures are also possible. Dampness, for example, can cause the Qi-flow to move too slowly. However internal factors can also play a role in causing harmful, excessive Qi, for instance, when the human senses get over-stimulated or have too many emotions. These causes produce local obstructions and thus result in disharmony of the Qi-flow. This ultimately leads to ailments and illnesses. On the other end, depleted Qi is also harmful, and causes the behavior of the person to become more nervous and anxious. The outcome of depleted Qi is a tense Qi-flow, caused by the decrease in volume, and density of Qi causes this. For example, a patient who has suffered from illness for a long period of time often has depleted Qi. In other words, the activity of the flow of this Qi is, in comparison, lower than in healthy persons, and the concentration of Qi is smaller in one or another body part.

By illustrating how Qi-exchange works, the concept of Qi-flow will be more evident. Take a fluid-filled sack kept under water for example, where the sack is made from a semi-permeable membrane. This sack is a metaphor for the physical human body, and the mentioned fluid will be referring to the Qi-flow inside the body. The membrane of the sack allows water to pass through. In order to allow water through the sack, it has to pass the membrane. If water passes through the sack smoothly in one direction, free from obstructions, without disturbing the natural flow of the fluid inside, then this Qi-flow is called "upright Qi" or "proper Qi." "Deviant Qi" behaves the opposite way. Water passes through the sack and confuses the natural flow of the fluid inside the sack. In other words, the external (water outside the sack) and internal (fluid inside the sack) flows are not in harmony with each other. So the purpose of healing is about correcting the Qi-flow.

By examining the example of the sack, we can metaphorically derive that the sack acts as a microcosm (the human body is viewed as a miniature universe with mountain, ocean, river and reservoir) within the macrocosm (big container universe). Namely, the water outside the sack plays as the macrocosm and the sack itself as the microcosm. When we translate this to the human body, we find that the body functions in a similar fashion. The human body, metaphor to the microcosm, has a close and dynamic relation with its environment, metaphor to macrocosm. Free travel, inward and outward movement of Qi, and adequate blood flow, mean the absence of disorders in the body. This free travel and movement are comparable to the correct Qi-flow. In short, the body is a dynamic system in interaction with the cosmos where the degree of Qi-permeability and right Qi-flow is of right concern. The *Huangdi neijing taisu* 黃帝內經太素 describes the Qi-penetration through the body as follows:

"Since ancient times it has been understood that penetration by the Qi of heaven is the basis of life, which depends on the universal Qi of yin and yang. The Qi of everything in the midst of heaven and earth and in the six directions, from the nine provinces and nine body orifices to the five visceral systems and the twelve joints, is penetrated by the Qi of heaven."

However, this penetration is not that obscure. From a Daoist point of view, the body receives Qi mainly from pure food/water consumption, fresh air inhalation and sunlight absorption. For sustaining human life, the body can neither be totally open nor totally closed, meaning that food and Qi enter the body and this naturally prevents agents of the disease from getting into the vital system. Also, wastes must be excreted without losing vital resources of the body. Agents of disease might enter the body via the bodily orifices, but the pores of the skin over the whole body are actually more vulnerable to it. The tightness of the pores and orifices has a close relation to the vulnerability of the body to outside disorders as well. Knowing this has great consequences for both prevention and therapy. When agents of feverish disorders, just penetrated into the body, for example, using a sudorific to force them back through the pores with perspiration is a remedy. So keeping healthy fluids in and excreting unhealthy substances is a part of maintaining good health.

Immortality With a Capital 'I'

In summary, we can state that the manifestation of health is the result of a good balance in the dynamics of body processes and that illness is an imbalance of it. Basically, a healthy body is indispensable for spiritual progress. At least bodily suffering is greatly diminished or completely vanquished. Many Daoist physical exercises not only have health benefits and positive influence on the mind, but bodily bliss is often a by-product from personal experience. This bliss is higher and different in nature than a lower and inferior type of pleasure of senses. So a spiritual practitioner may raise their consciousness at least from lower pleasures to higher bodily bliss. However, we must remember that bodily bliss, similar to pleasure, also comes and fades away.

Traditional Daoist spiritual self-cultivation and physical exercises aspire not only for healthy body and mind (non-existent or greatly reduced bodily suffering accompanied with clear mental mind), but also living harmoniously on earth with general happiness through contentment. But foremost is its focus on becoming a Daoist immortal/god in heavenly abode of bliss after finite human existence expires. The Daoist path described in this article is a path of Qi control, accumulation of Qi, moving Qi, and transformation from gross to subtlest states, i.e., transformation in stages of vital essence, Qi, shen – spirit to emptiness and primordial unity with the Dao.

The general view and final goal of the Daoist path, although different lineages over varying periods of time may sport different views, is not only obviating the death-event, but also to attain an exalted state of existence through attaining to higher realities. Self-cultivation as in transforming jing, Qi, and shen, can be viewed as a process of personal purification, and to also a way to gain an enhanced awareness of reality. Once the transformation process is complete, immortality could well become more readily understood, i.e., one will not be extinguished when the physical body dies. Daoist immortalism, and Chinese *xian* 仙 /*xianren* 仙人, have a strong connection to the heavenly god. Therefore, the path to heavenly state of *xianren* can be called celestial immortality.

According to Prof. Dr. Stephen Eskildsen in *The teachings and practices of the Early Quanzhen Taoist Masters*: "*For the Quanzhen masters, an Immortal was a spiritually enlightened person in complete control of his body and its fate who possessed various super-normal qualities and who had the compassion and power to bring great benefits to others. The Immortal conceived of by Wang and his followers would undergo the inevitable death of the physical body, but upon his or her death would have a refined yang spirit that would ascend into an everlasting, deified existence.*"

The *yang* spirit is Immortality itself and refers to the One. The One is the principle of the Dao, and It exists inside all people, and in matter. The One can be realized merely within oneself without seeking outwardly. The *yang* spirit survives after the death of the physical body and could be sent in and out of the body at will. Also, by transcending a life of mere mundane existence, a qualified adept could instead exert tremendous power. The Daoist and Taijiquan master, Sun Lutang 孫祿堂 (1860-1933), predicted the date of his physical death and departure from the body, and left the body at will during deep meditation. In other words, the *yang* spirit is Immortal and possesses omnipotent power, but it has to be manifested by self-cultivation, by circulating, retaining, and refining the Qi through various spiritual practices. The entire aspect of this inner physiological transformation theory and its methods is, for a large part, unique to Daoism.

Contrarily, in an interview with Wudang Quanzhen Sanfeng branch 武當 全真三豐派, Daoist head-master Zhong Yunlong's 鐘雲龍 view on immortality is that it is not something concerning only the afterlife, but is simply about explaining how a spiritual aspirant reaches his/her full potential in their present life, and realizing that their ability for creative expression is unlimited.

In addition, attaining supernatural powers or immortality, and reaching blissful heaven, for a Daoist, is a worthy aspiration. To some Buddhists, such as Kūkai 空海 (774-835), even Daoist heavenly life is finite, and one should transcend this heavenly realm for true Immortality. Ultimate Liberation in Buddhist terms equates to Nirvana, full Enlightenment. It is believed by some, if not all Wudang Daoists, that one will come back to earth after a sojourn in the heavenly abode of bliss. Some Wudang Daoists are aware of the difference between traditional Daoism and Buddhism's ultimate goal, and they may strive for the latter at later stages of life.

The Quanzhen Daoist method of seated meditation called "seeing the nature" or *jianxing* 見性, is just one of the indicators that the Daoist sect borrowed from the many elements of Chinese Chan Buddhism. Both seek the salvation of the soul, to transcend mortality of the physical body in order to arrive at peace of mind, where the self is considered one with Dharma nature. However different, Quanzhen Daoist methods intrinsically are still Daoist in nature, meaning that the primary emphasis is, for example, placed upon the Daoist *Neidan* inner physiological transformation process and traditional religious Daoist rituals. Further, another major difference in seated meditation is the controlled breathing practice in Chan Buddhist meditation, which serves mainly as a way to clear and concentrate the mind, whereas in the Quanzhen Daoist meditation it is also a means to strengthen the body, while at the same time clearing and concentrating the mind.

However, I have to emphasize, theoretically and at a relative level the Daoist goal may appear different, but what truly happens in reality, only the practitioners know themselves. Many advanced Daoist practitioners are often hidden and have no interest in sharing complex esoteric Daoist knowledge and Ultimate Truth with the outside world. In real life, we simply cannot make 100% accurate conclusions, especially scholarly assumptions. This is why scholarly writing on spiritual subjects, in my opinion, almost always falls short, and never discloses the full spectrum of reality. Mere words pointing to truth are insufficient for conveying the whole truth. This can act as a reminder.

The Dao That Can be Cultivated is not Eternal Dao

Regarding Daoist inner self-cultivation and transformation, there is an interesting saying from Wudang mountain 'Quanzhen Xuanwu branch' 武當山全真 玄武派 and master You Xuande 游玄德. Chapter one of *Dao De Jing* 道德經 is often regarded as the most important and profound. Traditionally, *Dao De Jing* from You Xuande is recited differently from the ordinary version. The first chapter of the *Dao De Jing*, for example, is recited as: *"dao ke cheng dao, fei dao"* or 道可成道, 非道, meaning *"The Dao that can be cultivated is not the Eternal Dao."* He understood this short passage only at an older age, but he did not elaborate further on its meaning. Personally, the passage may be understood in terms of The Ultimate as follow: *"The Eternal is ever present and is Unborn, Immortal, beyond transformation of gain and loss. Therefore we should have detachment from the senses, along with the intellectual mind and ego, and realize our Consciousness, or Real Person/Self, which is Unlimited and Non-dual."* Apparently, the notion exists, at least within the Xuanwu branch of Wudang Daoists, that we

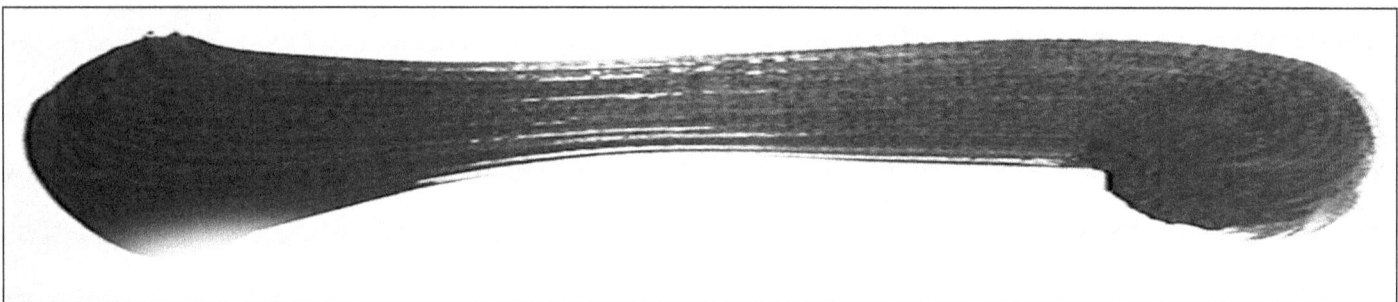

already have It. We only need to realize It and let go the concept of becoming It.

And so, the transformation of energies (Daoist inner self-cultivation) is only a path, not the end. Realizing Higher Truth sabotaged earlier spiritual practices and made them obsolete. Realizing this, then *wuwei* 無為 truly begins, being intentionally inactive. Knowing the Ultimate Dao cannot be gained through gathering and transformation of Qi; neither can it be lost.

Another notion and result of having finished Daoist self-cultivation are: when the individuals realize that their existence and consciousness are unreal, and one is completely free of conceptual and dualistic viewpoints, and feelings based on self-consciousness. Only then has one become a real part of the omnipotent, omnipresent single reality. Although the Quanzhen sect views the human body and consciousness as ultimately impermanent and illusory, however, when the human body and mind are harmoniously used together, it becomes the best possible apparatus to transcend the illusory world and return to the One and only, everlasting and unbounded, the omnipotent Dao.

Daoist Relation to Non-duality

During a dark retreat, Daoist master adept Zhong Yunlong 鐘雲龍, once shared his experience of seeing white light. Whether the white light is Non-dual or not remains unclear. Further, when human beings conceive Ultimate Truth, having glimpses of Non-duality, it is often seeing the Light (Non-dual White Light) or hearing It. Some hear true "inner" Mantra (esoteric Buddhism) or Primal Vibration (similar to Vedic AUM vibration). In Christian mysticism and The Gnostic Bible, and in the inner teachings of The Gospel of Thomas, The Gospel of John, The Gospel of Truth, The Gospel of Philip, and The book of Thomas, numerous mentions are made of The Light. Tibetan Buddhism at higher stages of realization also mentions about dwelling in clear light.

Another Wudang Longmen branch Daoist adept from Quanzhen Dragon Gate branch 武當山 全真龍門派, called Zhang Zhishun 張智順, also known as Mijingzi 米晶子, condensed the Daozang 道藏 or Daoist Canon (largest collection of Daoist texts) into essence and brought it out in a two-volume book called Wu Ti Yuan Liu 無體源流. The Daozang not only consists practical experiential advice on meditation, but also holds the majority of Chinese alchemical sources. Zhang Zhishun also shares his experience of hearing *"thunderous vibration like the falling of a hammer"* during deep meditation. Thus, from two great Wudang Daoist masters, namely Zhong Yunlong and Zhang Zhishun, we can bring forth and assume, at a certain advanced level of practice), that the outcome of seeing light and hearing vibration may be very similar to that of other spiritual traditions. This could mean — although the Daoist path differs from other spiritual traditions — that at the highest spiritual stage, perhaps Non-duality experiences may be similar.

Simultaneous Cultivation of Daoism and Chinese Buddhism

Hu Xuezhi 胡學志, as a senior Wudang Longmen branch Daoist adept and friend of mine, authored several books about Daoist neidan, including *Revealing the Tao Te Ching: In-Depth Commentaries on an Ancient Classic*, and *Discourse on Chuang Tzu: Expounding on the Dream of a Butterfly vol. I and II*. From the latter, in vol. I, he states *"When there is ego, I am in heaven and earth. When there is no ego, heaven and earth are within me. When all defilements are completely cleansed, the absolute origin of all reveals itself unreservedly, and thus, once again, the simple and pure innate nature can rest upon its primeval source! How is that achieved? By 'forgetting' and putting aside the ego and external objects, and reverting to absolute independence. Thus, for he whose mind holds the intent to transform himself into a 'True Man', he need only abide in concentration, within simplicity and purity, in order to combine his intent with the 'intent' of Great Nature."*

He also greatly studies Chinese Buddhist scriptures and visits Chinese Buddhist hermits and true practitioners. In what he terms as dual cultivation, we both share the same view, in short: Chinese Buddhism is very clear on analysis of mind, or mind training (less mental and emotional suffering), to transcend the world and get beyond the cycle of rebirth. Whereas Daoism specializes in survival (minimize bodily suffering and harm from outside influences), cultivating corporeal body and understanding of the inner cosmos (human body) and outer cosmos (this world of duality, five elements, geomancy, cosmology, astrology, etc.) or basically the universe that human beings inhabit. To understand the world of duality and its myriad manifestations, Yijing/I Ching 易經 or Book of Changes, is an important Chinese divination text. For this I recommend my teacher, Prof. Dennis Cheng Kat-Hung 鄭吉雄 and his in-depth Yijing version, only available in Chinese language 易詮釋中的儒道互動. Thus, Chinese Buddhism and Daoism together are complementary in terms of one cultivating corporeal body laying a foundation for the higher study of mind.

A Way to Complement Chinese Buddhism with Daoism

Chinese Chan Buddhist and Quanzhen Daoist practices may vary and differ in nature. For practitioners, it is advisable to have a single main path of practice. Otherwise, stagnant spiritual progress or confusion may arise. Traditional Buddhist or traditional Daoist practices or exercises should be done separately. For instance, main Buddhist practice with Daoist complementary elements could be as follows: Buddhist devotion (mantra/sutra recitation), scriptural study, mindfulness/awareness (being in present moment, watch the mind) and Chan Buddhist zhengti li 整體力 or whole body mechanical strength based exercises. These can safely and effectively be complemented with:

1. Safe Daoist health-oriented physical exercises with non-intentional/non-moving Qi-circulation involved, such as "eight pieces of brocade." 2. Daoist modern Xuanxue/xiandai Xuanxue 現代玄學 (in China often in short, Xuanxue) or practical knowledge on daily living, as Fengshui geomancy and astrology/cosmology related matter. 3. Daoist philosophy and scriptural study. 4. Traditional Chinese Medicine. 5. Daoist musical instruments such as Chinese zither or guqin 古琴. 6. Daoist arts, such as painting, calligraphy and poetry writing.

For instance, my Xuanxue teacher Master Peter So Man-fung 蘇民峰, is privately a Tibetan Buddhist Gelug Lamrim practitioner, but he teaches and does Xuanxue advice publicly as a way of living. Thus, variations of Buddhism together with Daoist elements do occur. Further, personal Xuanxue curriculum consists of Fengshui geomancy風水學, xingming xue 姓名學 or knowledge of person's name, mianxiang 面相學 or facial reading, zhangxiang 掌相學 palm reading, and bazi mingli 八字命理學. Latter Art of Divination that practically calculates a person's postnatal human character, behavior, temperament, and inclination toward certain personal likes and dislikes. Xuanxue knowledge is often used in Daoist folk religious Chinese fortune telling. In my opinion, however, if cleverly utilized in daily life, it is a way of understanding the lower self and knowledge of how to avoid suffering and calamities from external factors. Understanding the lower self is not the real Self. It can help in understanding the human ego. In other words, knowing what is at least not true self will aid in finding real Self.

In relation to Confucius Analects, or Lunyu 論語 we find, "Zi yue子曰: ke ji fu li wei ren克己復禮為仁," meaning: *"The Master said, 'To subdue one's self and return to propriety is perfect virtue.'"* My definition, or its Daoist inner meaning is; *"keji fu zhen wei dao"* 克己復真為道, meaning, to subdue one's lower self and return to the Real (Self) is the (Ultimate) Path. As the American Daoist Liu Ming (Charles Belyea) would confirm, Confucianism and Daoism are really two sides of the same coin.

The Dao in Confucianism

Confucius (551-479 B.C.) is most well-known as a Chinese philosopher, establishing principally an ethics and morality school of thought (a method to govern and to lead with the aim to bring Confucian self-cultivation, human order in the family, organize society, and pacify the nation) known as Confucianism or Ruism, Rujia 儒家, in Chinese. In China, he was also named as Kongzi 孔子, Kong Fuzi 孔夫子, Kong Qiu 孔丘 (given name at birth), or Zhongni 仲尼 (adult name). The Four Books, or Sishu 四書, are classic Chinese texts selected by Confucian scholar Zhu Xi 朱熹 (1130–1200). The Four Books, namely *The Great Learning* or Daxue 大學, *The Analects of Confucius* or Lunyu 論語, *Mencius* or Mengzi 孟子, and *The Doctrine of the Mean* or Zhongyong 中庸 (this more mystical spiritual classic formed a bridge between Daoism and Chinese Buddhism), represent the core values and belief systems of Confucius.

Although Daoism and Confucianism both use the word Dao, the Confucian interpretation of the Dao is not entirely similar. In the Far East Chinese-English Dictionary or 遠東漢英大辭典, we find the translation of the word 道 Dao as –

1. A road, a path, a street
2. The "way" (in the metaphysical sense)
3. A way, a method
4. Daoism, a Daoist
5. To say, to speak
6. An administrative district in old China
7. A theory, a doctrine
8. To govern, to lead
9. To think, to suppose
10. A skill, an art, a craft
11. A Chinese family name

An important interpretation of 道 Dao/Tao in the early Daoist context (Laozi Dao De Jing) could be clarified from my Universal Daoist (Yiguandao) colleague, Derek Lin in his Tao Te Ching Annotated & Explained, in chapter one:

"The Tao that can be spoken is not the eternal Tao. The name that can be named is not the eternal name. The nameless is the origin of Heaven and Earth. The named is the mother of myriad things…What it actually means is that we can never understand the Tao through the intellect alone…Not only is the Tao beyond the power of spoken words to describe, but it is also beyond the power of written words to define. That which can be defined is limited by the definition, and the Tao transcends all limitations…Therefore, the Tao that initiated Creation was the ultimate nameless enigma…."

Confucian use and definition of the word Dao/Tao compared to Daoism, according to prof. Wing-Tsit Chan 陳榮捷 (1901-1994) is here taken from A sourcebook in Chinese philosophy: *"In no other Confucian work (Doctrine of the Mean) is the Way (Tao) given such a central position. This self-directing Way seems to be the same as the Tao in Taoism. But the difference is great.*

As Ch'ien Mu has pointed out, when the Taoists talk about Tao as being natural, it means that Tao is void and empty, whereas when Confucianists talk about Tao as being natural, they describe it as sincerity. This, according to him, is a great contribution of the Doctrine of the Mean. It should also be pointed out that with Confucianists, 'The Way is not far from man.' Contrary to the Tao of Taoism, the Confucian Tao is strongly humanistic."

The Confucian Dao in *The Four Books* aforementioned mostly refers to the way as in a path of method/doctrine, to lead/govern people in Confucian ethical codes and moral values. Nevertheless, in "*The Analects,*" chapter five, verse 13, we find this mentioning of Tiandao or "way of heaven" (sinologist James Legge translation): "*Zi Gong said, 'The Master's personal displays of his principles and ordinary descriptions of them may be heard. His discourses about man's nature, and the way of Heaven, cannot be heard.'*"

In my opinion, the Daoist Dao is mystical and metaphysical in nature, and Confucius could have known of it (Laozi and Confucius probably had met each other), but he would have not found it the right time to share higher wisdom with common people. According to Wing-Tsit Chan in a sourcebook in Chinese philosophy: "*Human nature, endowed by Heaven, is revealed through the states of equilibrium and harmony, which are themselves the 'condition of the world' and the 'universal path.' The Way of Heaven transcends time, space, substance, and motion, and is at the same time eternal, and evident.*"

Moreover, Confucius elaborates on Tiandao and relates it to Daoist term Wuwei in *The Book of Rites*, or *Liji*, in chapter 哀公問, Ai Gong Wen, verse 12:

"*The duke said, 'I venture to ask what it is that the superior man values in the way of Heaven.' Confucius replied, 'He values its unceasingness (incessantly, endlessly). There is, for instance, the succession and sequence of the sun and moon from the east and west – that is the way of Heaven. There is the long continuance of its progress without interruption – that is the way of Heaven. There is its making (all) things complete without doing anything (Wuwei 無為) – that is the way of Heaven. There is their brilliancy when they have been completed – that is the way of Heaven.'*"

More clearly, in the Discourse on Chuang Tzu: *Expounding on the Dream of a Butterfly* vol. I, p.285: "*Manifested in heaven and earth, Tao becomes the Way of heaven. Never pausing, it eternally endures, following its revolving course through every epoch, and uniformly prevailing throughout myriads of phenomena, free from all hindrance.*" In other words, Tiandao in the Book of Rites refers not only to sincerity and self-directing, but also to the Daoist notion of naturalness, Wuwei and eternity. Thus, Daoist Dao 道 and the Confucian Tiandao 天道 are very close in meaning, if not referring to exactly the same thing.

Final remarks

One may notice the close relationship Quanzhen Daoism has with Chinese Chan Buddhism in certain areas. I would like to emphasize, the Quanzhen Daoist path and Chinese Chan Buddhist path use different methods. My suggestion is to choose the path which suits the individuals character, temperament and interest. I will make a comment here on Daoist physical exercises, guqin, painting, and calligraphy. From experience, Daoist practices often take a long time to learn, study and often a lifetime to master. Chan Buddhist physical exercises and arts are often taken in their essence, being less complex, more efficient, and more direct, and with a lower learning curve and shorter time to master, while still being effective.

Also Chan Buddhist theme music or painting can be much more minimalistic in character, but still profound when the corresponding philosophy is understood. As one learns to read, personal inclination moves slowly from pure traditional Daoist practices to principally Chinese Chan Buddhist practices. In my opinion, Chan Buddhist practices may be suited to people with less time, or people wanting a more direct and efficient type of spiritual approach, though not compromising in quality of practice. Of course, selecting the main path is related to personal needs, interest, temperament, character, compatibility with living surrounding, practice in solitude or under the guidance, and most importantly, in what direction the heart is headed. As long as we walk our path consistently, the True Path and direction will be shown. For example, the master finds the disciple and not another way around. Certain spiritual experiences as a type of guide on the path do exist.

Personally, I appreciate the Quanzhen Daoist their openmindedness towards other religious ideas, dedication, investigation, innovation, individual effort, and severe self-discipline. I also cherish their attitude of proto-science toward Truth in general; examination and practice through trial and error, seeking the essential, room for new developments in doctrine and practice, and verification of certain methods for why they would work for an individual.

In conclusion, the Quanzhen master their path towards enlightenment and Immortal-hood through a characteristically physiological alchemical process, as well as a spiritual one. *Dantian* have to be cultivated. Cultivating the three *dantian* and transforming energies (unless it is your path) is an arduous, potentially harmful, and long journey. Success is not guaranteed. There are some safe Daoist health exercises though, as mentioned in the beginning. Along with Zhang Zhishun's external aspect practice of the "eight pieces of diamond practice," one should also exercise his internal aspect practice – as in *yin-yang* balance, *chang shou gong* 長壽功 or Immortality/Longevity practice.

Zhang Zhishun advises us to practice immovable *xiantian Qi* 先天之氣 and not what most people nowadays are doing, namely practicing movable *houtian Qi* 後天之氣. He warns us about practicing movable *houtian Qi*, since the whole body may get into problems. So, the path of working with energies, as in the transformation of *jing*, Qi, and *shen*, is only for the selected few, in my opinion. Even under the guidance of an experienced teacher one should proceed with caution. Other paths like devotion, *mantra/sutra* recitation, singing spiritual songs, scriptural study, concentration, mindfulness (as in watching the mind), or expression in spiritual art forms are, in my viewpoint, totally safe — especially under the guidance of a teacher.

Lastly, everyone is born with *chakras*, but not everyone is born with *dantian* 丹田. Three points of dantian may overlap certain *chakra* points, but are not the same. With this in mind, why not focus effort on what we already have inside?

> Start practice along with scriptural study
> Spiritual experiences may come unexpectedly
> Rationally we may choose a certain path
> But our heart may say otherwise
> Keep walking consistently and with sincerity
> The Path will be unveiled miraculously
>
> Stop trying to find out why and how the revelations appear
> Phenomena & Non-duality can not be explained in totality
> That which is revealed will become closest to our heart
> Unshakable and unmovable faith
> With certainty
>
> This is true insurance when passing from the body
> Memorization of holy words is not truly knowing
> Only Inner Knowledge of Highest Truth is
> Mere intellectual knowledge and endless research
> Many still never truly believe
> Disciplined practice will bear its fruits
> Only this removes all doubt,
> and one will have no choice but to believe It is Real

Lam FuHo 林富豪 is a Universalist and sinologist. Often called the 'Uomo Universale' for his expressions generally in music, painting, and poetry, he believes the concept of Uomo Universale has similarities with the Daoist concept of self-cultivation — mental and physical self-improvement as well as spiritual practice through the arts. His intellectual interests are in Advaita Vedanta and Christian mysticism. Daily practices are from Daoism and Buddhism.

Select Quotes: The Wisdom of Lao-Tzu

Watch your thoughts; they become words.
Watch your words; they become actions.
Watch your actions; they become habits.
Watch your habits; they become character.
Watch your character;
it becomes your destiny.

To lead people, walk behind them.

Violence, even well intentioned, always rebounds upon oneself.

What the caterpillar calls the end, the rest of the world calls a butterfly.

Care about what other people think and you will always be their prisoner.

Only fools seek power, and the greatest fools seek it through force.

Give a man a fish and you feed him for a day. Teach him how to fish and you feed him for a lifetime.

◆ RABBI RAMI SHAPIRO

GREAT IS PEACE
Peace in the Jewish Tradition

FOR ME to write of peace when so much of my world is burning with hate is either an act of extreme chutzpah (daring), frustration, or futility — maybe a bit of all three. As a rabbi I am simultaneously frightened and ashamed by the acts behind the headlines that lay on my doorstep each morning. I shake my head in despair as two of the world's greatest spiritual traditions are perverted to fuel hatred that both decry. I want to be able to offer a solution to the evil that haunts us. I want to turn to my tradition and find a way to peace that would put an end to war. And there is much from which to draw. Judaism, no less than any other faith, rests on the profound understanding of the innate sanctity of human life. But in the end I cannot find in these words the solace I need or the solution I desire.

Perhaps, however, my problem is that I am looking for something grand when in fact the solution and hope lay elsewhere. Perhaps the truth is quite simple and the solution quite plain. Perhaps the hate and violence that makes the headlines is simply the hate and violence that rests in our own hearts. Perhaps the international is not really other than the interpersonal; and the interpersonal not really other than the personal. Perhaps the only solution lies in my heart and in yours. Perhaps it is not about them, but me; not about what they should do, but what we can do. Perhaps.

So with this caveat I turn to my tradition. The rabbis tell us that God created a single human being to remind us of our common ancestry. We are, all of us, cousins. And to remind us that in our singularity we can bring about a revolution that may impact the entire family.

To see what one person can do I turned to the Talmud, the 2500 year old compendium of rabbinic insight and teaching. In the Vilna edition of the Talmud we find appended to the ten chapters of tractate Derekh Eretz [The Way of the World] an eleventh chapter called Perek HaShalom, the Chapter of Peace. Nothing is known of this chapter. Its authorship and date are a mystery. Why it is attached to Derekh Eretz also is unknown. All that we know is that this chapter is a collection of teachings on the centrality of peace. Coming as it does immediately after a long series of teachings on how to live life with justice and compassion, we can surmise that the editors of the Vilna edition of the Talmud saw Perek HaShalom as a fitting addendum to Derekh Eretz.

Regardless of its history, however, Perek HaShalom is a powerful collection of millennia-old rabbinic teachings on peace. For our purposes here, I shall share selections from the text accompanied by short commentary. My goal is twofold: first, to make clear the centrality of peace in the Jewish worldview; and second to offer an ancient and timeless practice that may transform your heart and our world. Just as God began the human race with one person, so may we transform it with one person as well: ourself.

Rabbi Joshua ben Levi said: Great is Peace, for peace is to the world as leaven is to dough. Without peace the world is flat, brittle, lifeless. Peace is what allows life to rise above fear. Without it we are in a constant state of high anxiety, hiding from each other, and lacking the basic trust needed to create civilization and community.

Rabban Simeon ben Gamaliel used to say: By three things does the world endure: justice, truth and peace. Rabbi Muna taught: These three are in truth one, for when justice is done truth is revealed and peace established. Wherever justice is done peace is found. Rabban Gamaliel saw justice, truth, and peace as separate pillars upon which the world rests. Rabbi Muna saw justice as more foundational. Without justice neither truth nor peace could survive. What then is justice? Justice is treating each other with the recognition that we are each and all children of the One who manifests the many. Justice is the recognition of our true nature as the image and likeness of God. When we know the truth of who we are, we cannot help but engage each other in peace.

Hezekiah said: Great is Peace, for of all the commandments only peace is unconditional: seek peace and pursue it [Psalm 34:15]. This means we are to seek it in the place we are and bring it to the place we are going. Throughout the Torah the Israelites are taught the commandments conditional to specific situations: "If you see" [Exodus 23:5]; "If you meet" [Exodus 23:4]; "If you build" [Deuteronomy 22:8], but with regard to peace there are no conditions. We are to make peace regardless of the situation in which we find ourselves. We are to seek peace and pursue it. Seek it here and now. And pursue it in the future.

At first this seems redundant, for if I have established peace in the present I will have established it in the Eternal Present. The future is an illusion, a projection. This is true from the absolute perspective of God, but from the relative perspective of people and nations there is history and destiny. If I establish peace now I must still pursue it tomorrow. Indeed, it is only when we have made peace between us now that we can together pursue an even greater peace tomorrow.

Hezekiah also taught: Great is Peace, for throughout their wanderings Torah speaks of the Israelites in the plural implying dissension, but when they come to Sinai Torah speaks of them as one. It was then that the Holy One, blessed be He, said: "Because Israel has come to hate violence and love peace, and in this way become one, this is the time when I shall give them My Torah." What an amazing teaching! Hezekiah is saying that in order to merit the Teaching of Peace [the Torah], the people must have already established peace. The Torah becomes a confirmation of what is and not just a call to what can be. Thus, when the Torah calls us to be peaceful, she is simply calling us to our true nature, urging us to do what is already in our power to do. We do not need God's help to bring peace; we need God to remind us that we already know how to be peaceful. Hezekiah is saying that there is no path to peace but only paths that are already peaceful. You cannot move from strife to peace, you can only be established in peace here and now.

Great is Peace, for Rabbi Judah, the Prince, said: "It is forbidden to lie except for the purpose of making peace between one person and another." Here Rabbi Judah suggests peace is more important than truth, and takes precedence over it. Rabban Simeon ben Gamaliel supports Rabbi Judah's insight with this story from the life of Aaron, Moses' brother and High Priest of Israel:

Rabbi Simeon ben Gamaliel said: Great is Peace, for Aaron the High Priest was praised only for peace; for he loved peace, pursued peace, greeted people with peace, and responded to their greetings with peace. Of him the Holy One, blessed be He, says "He walked with Me in peace" [Malachi 2:6]. If Aaron noticed two people quarreling he would go to the first and claim that the second is repentant and distraught over the quarrel, and then go to the second claiming the same about the first; in this way he encouraged each to reach out to the other in peace. This was how Aaron established peace, love, and friendship among the people. Aaron is the Jewish role model of the peacemaker. Elsewhere in the teachings of the rabbis there is a story of a husband and wife who are having a heated argument. The husband vows not to make peace with his wife until she spits in the eye of Aaron the High Priest. As soon as he said it he regretted his words, but felt bound by them nonetheless. Hearing of the couple's plight, Aaron sought out the wife. "There is something in my eye," he said to her, "and I cannot get it out. If you would be so kind as to spit in my eye I am sure the irritant would flow out." The woman did as she was asked, and then returned home to her contrite husband. If the High Priest can be humble enough to allow someone to spit in his eye in the cause of peace, we who are of a far lesser stature should do no less.

So how are we to seek peace and pursue it? Perek HaShalom offers some practical advice again based on Aaron.

Rabbi Hiyya ben Abba said: "Great is Peace, for one who loves peace and pursues peace, should welcome all people with greetings of peace and respond to their greetings with peace, and maintain peace between Israel and their Father in heaven, this one is surely called Peace." And Rabbi Joshua of Siknin taught: "Great is Peace, for all you who love peace, pursue peace, and give greetings of peace, and respond to the greetings of others with peace, the Holy One, blessed be He, will cause you to inherit life in this world and life in the World to Come."

What is it that these teachers say is the key to seeking peace and pursuing it? Greeting and responding to each other with words of peace. They mean literally to open and close our conversations with the Hebrew word shalom, peace. Is this all there is to it? Can this one word bracketing our conversations really establish peace between people?

While I do not want to oversimplify the challenge of peace, I do think these sages are on to something. They are not talking about world peace, or peace talks between nations. They are addressing peace talk between people. If we address each other in peace at all times, peace would reign at all times. Without seeking to find flaws in their reasoning by expanding the idea to nations, let us see what the impact might be when applied to individuals.

When greeting someone with Shalom we are setting both awareness and intention. The awareness comes from the meaning of Shalom. Shalom comes from the Hebrew root sh-l-m which it shares with the word Shalem, wholeness. Peace is the recognition of the wholeness of which all beings are a part. When I greet someone with "Shalom" I am acknowledging our interdependence and our mutuality in God. Shalom as peace does not mean we cannot engage in conflict, but that we cannot do so with the illusion that we are independent of one another. There are legitimate things over which we can disagree and struggle, but we must always do so mindful of the fact that neither of us can win the battle unless both of us win. What appears to be a win for one at the expense of another is in fact a loss for both.

The Talmud illustrates this with a story of two men in a boat. One man begins to drill a hole under his seat. The other argues with him to stop. "What matter is it of yours," the first man asks. "This is my seat and I can do with it as I please." The absurdity of the statement, given that they are literally in the same boat, illustrates the rabbis' position that we are each responsible for the welfare of the other.

Similarly, when we depart from a person and leave them with words of "Shalom," we reestablish our awareness of our unity and interdependence. Even a conversation that contains much strife ends with a shared affirmation of peace and wholeness, seeing to it that actions resulting from that conversation will honor the one boat we all share.

I am not saying that greeting each other with mindfulness will solve all the problems in the world. But I am saying, as did my teachers thousands of years before me, that it can establish the awareness we need to seek peace and pursue it.

Shalom.

Rabbi Rami Shapiro is an award-winning author, poet, essayist, and educator whose poems have been anthologized in over a dozen volumes, and whose prayers are used in prayer books around the world. Rami received rabbinical ordination from the Hebrew Union College–Jewish Institute of Religion and holds doctoral degrees in both Jewish studies and divinity. A congregational rabbi for 20 years, Rabbi Shapiro currently teaches Religious Studies at Middle Tennessee State University, and directs One River (**www.one-river.org**), a not-for-profit educational foundation devoted to building community through contemplative conversation. Rami writes a regular column for Spirituality and Health Magazine called Roadside Assistance on Your Spiritual Journey. His most recent books are The Sacred Art of Lovingkindness, The Divine Feminine, and Open Secrets from which this essay was adapted. Rabbi Rami can be reached through his website, **www.rabbirami.com**

◆ SHEIKH NUR AL-JERRAHI

The Mystical Power of Islam
On the Sublime Secrets and Nondual Philosophy of the World's Youngest Religious Tradition

These precious words on the religion of Islam, which is still hardly understood in this day and time, profess the true spirit of what is termed "Mohammedism" among the major religious traditions of the world. They were spoken over the course of two programs by Lex Hixon (later to become known as Sheikh Nur Al-Jerrahi) on the radio show Body, Mind, Spirit, *on 3/19/80, and 6/23/80. These two programs have been coalesced to form this article. Selected* suras *from the Holy Koran, translated and transmitted by him, as well as dreams and insights of the then ardent Muslim practitioner, have been culled out and gathered as well.*

I have had the good fortune in my life of taking hand with Sheikh Muzafer Effendi and entering his *taricot*, his order, and spending a month with him and his dervishes during the month of Ramadan, in Istanbul two summers ago. In this way I received a living transmission through my pores and through my cells, not just through reading books or newspapers, or watching television, which is the way that most of us gain any idea of what the tradition of Islam is all about — which is a totally distorted one.

Sheihk Muzzafer is the nineteenth in succession of a line of Sheiks from a great, remarkable saint, Pir Nurredin Jerrahi, who passed in 1721, and the lore reaches very, very far back into the ancient ways of the Turkish people, as well as reflecting the mystical power of authentic Islam.

There are 750 million Muslims in the world at present. They are everywhere; they are in every country. Recently, the New York Times printed some sort of map which showed the distribution of Muslims in the world. Typical of the New York Times, they did not include mention of the many Muslims here in the United States. The United States has a rich tradition of Islam, with many devotees living and practicing here, and it will become richer when beings like Sheikh Muzafer Effendi visits. He is coming to New York with some of his dervishes in a few days for the first time, and spending a couple of weeks in the city, performing Dzikr and speaking on and answering questions about the rich heritage of Islam.

Many people in the world still hold the erroneous idea that Islam is just a sort of rustic, desert tribe kind of religion. We have to remember that Islam formed the setting for some of the greatest civilizations that the world has known, the great sciences, the great arts and architecture — what to speak of many of the great mystics. How little we know about it and its scriptures, and how for hundreds of years Western countries such as Spain and Russia have been avenues through which this youngest of all religions is growing, and sending its substantial wisdom out to the world.

To be more precise, and to get to the point of some of the issues around Islam, this idea that Islam spreads through the propagation of Holy War, is really repulsive. I must say that I base my own understanding of Islam upon living in a dervish community in Istanbul, communing with the people there, feeling the peace and the love among them, and particularly, the true nonviolence of these dervish people.

So, the idea of Holy War is something I find repulsive, but other than just Islam, this base idea permeates all religion and all political bodies, and individual minds as well. In Islam, one of the points of spirituality, a real religious practice — not just a formal or conventional one, but a real one — is to actually burn away all such notions as a Holy War. One is to take it out of one's heart and mind, and out of the culture as well.

Here it can be said, that to get an idea of what Islam is really like from radical terrorists that call themselves Muslims is like trying to get an idea of what the Quaker religion is like from ex-President Nixon, who was a Quaker at one time. Thus, if one really wants to get the idea of what a spiritual path is, you must go to the people who are immersed in it and who are living it day to day, all their lives, and who are not bringing or allowing some sort of political distortions to bear upon it.

Therefore, the important thing to stress to people about Islam today is that to taste the sweetness and feel the power of Allah through the practice of the daily prayers, and through the friendship of the faithful, is crucial. In the body of the faithful there is an intense friendship — there is such a friendship in Islam that I have never felt in any other spiritual tradition. That is the kind of thing that people must feel for themselves, and then they can begin to start evaluating the matter from a historical context.

About the historical context, I feel that Islam can be so important to the world today. First of all, it is seven-hundred years younger than Christianity; it the youngest of the major religions that are around, so it is still vibrant. It has not been desecrated by European science, and by all manner of other points of view. It is still whole. It is intensely in touch with the earth. Another way of putting this is that Islam has always been here. Abraham was really one of the first Prophets, and Adam could be called the original prophet of Islam. Thus, there is a beautiful wholeness and integratedness to Islam.

With this introduction, I want to share some of the actual wisdom of the Koran. The words that you are about to hear are from the opening *sura* of the Koran, the Fatiha, that the practicing Muslim chants some forty times a day:

My beloved Mohammed:
Please teach people to pray in this way.

*May the spontaneous praise
arising from the hearts of all beings
be offered to Allah alone,
the ever-present Source of being,
the source of love flowing constantly
with the sweet balm of compassion and forgiveness.*

*This ultimate Source draws beings to their day of Truth,
their homecoming into the radiance of Allah.
To Allah alone, as the source of being,
can beings truly offer their entire being.
From Allah alone, as the source of power and love,
can beings receive authentic strength and guidance.*

*May Allah teach human beings how to turn consciously
toward their ever-present Source.
This is the direct path of Islam, taken by lovers of love
straight into the Source of Love.
This is not one of the paths
that wander endlessly through creation,
taken by all who turn away from the Source of creation.*

Source, alone is worthy of worship?'" Joyously, the soul replies: "Such a one is counted among the blessed, and after death awakens immediately into Paradise." "Good," replies the guide. "And since all souls are rays from the Light of Allah, the essence of every being Is this affirmation, that Allah alone is worthy of worship, and all beings awaken after the sleep of death, directly into Paradise.

The soul is exhilarated by this profound explanation, but because of its deep commitment to the words of the Holy Koran, it still hesitates to except the Truth that there is no separate realm called hell. The beloved guide sees this hesitation, and offers the soul the final solution to its doubts.

"My dear friend: It is true that when a soul who has not practiced a life of loving submission to Allah reaches Paradise, it cannot bear the intense radiance here, so it falls asleep again, and dreams of hell. Hellfire is simply the purifying radiance of Paradise. And all dreams, even dreams of eternal hell, are but momentary. These dreaming souls soon awaken to Paradise, fully purified, and joyously praising the All-Merciful One."

The explanation now complete, the soul feels the full coherence and power of the marvelous Truth of the all-merciful nature of Allah. However, this mystical teaching deepens the soul's longing to understand completely, and almost at once a profound question arises.

> "....this idea that Islam spreads through the propogation of Holy War is really repulsive. I base my own understanding of Islam upon living in a dervish community in Istanbul, communing with the people there, feeling the peace and the love among them, and particularly, the true nonviolence of these dervish people."

I have always had a deep curiosity about souls who wander away from the path and get lost, and what traditional religions say about such beings in their scriptures. When I joined the Jerrahi order and met my Sheikh, I began to have dreams of a deep kind, some of them which answered my lifelong curiosity around Heaven and hell. The following words relate one of those dreams I had, that I put down on paper:

The soul departs its earthly body and is taken in dream to Paradise. Led by a loving guide, it discovers Paradise to be vast, radiant gardens, filled with joyous beings of light who are engaged in countless forms of whirling, chanting, and silent forms of contemplation, called Dzikr — the constant remembrance of Allah.

Though overwhelmed by the beauty of Paradise, the soul desires to understand the whole picture and therefore asks its guide where the fires of hell are found. Smiling gently, the guide replies, "Dear friend: there is no separate realm that you call Hell."

The soul, steeped in the revelation of Islam, responds immediately: "But we read in the Holy Koran that those who deny Allah will suffer in hell, eternally." The beloved guide replies, firmly: "But you read also in the Holy Koran that Allah is all-compassionate and all-merciful. How could an all-compassionate power create a realm expressly designed for souls to suffer in, even for an instant, much less for eternity?"

This response startles and intrigues the soul, but it remains unconvinced. Perceiving this, the guide continues, asking. "What is taught in the mystic tradition about the person who, even once, repeats with utmost sincerity, 'La ilaha ill'allah — Allah , the ultimate

"My dear guide: If the experience of hell is just a dream, may not the experience of Paradise — its dancing maidens, its flowing streams, its radiant dervishes — may not all this be a dream as well?"

The guide responds with delight: "Ah, my dear, dear friend: You have guessed the secret. Paradise, too, is a dream. But it is Allah's perfect dream, totally unlike the fragmentary and confused dreams experienced by individual beings."

These words kindle the ecstasy of mystical knowledge in the soul, and it realizes that this insurpassable guide is none other than the prophet, Mohammed — may the peace and blessing of Allah always be upon him. And in this state of holy exaltation, the soul becomes bold enough to question the blessed Mohammed.

"Beloved guide, are you, too, a dream, telling me that hell and Paradise are dreams?"

The most excellent of guides responds instantly, and with great power:

"I am the dream-key, to the dream-lock, of the dream door that opens into the treasure of Divine Love, which alone is not a dream."

Through the spiritual potency of these words alone, that mystical door opens. The soul enters there and is lost in the treasure of Love. The dream of Paradise disappears. All that remains is the profound resonance of Allah's own Dzikr, the silent thunder of Allah! Allah! Allah! From this primordial, holy sound, all universes are being born, and into it they are disappearing again.

Suddenly, the soul finds itself once again in the radiant dream called divine Paradise. The beloved guide takes the soul in his arms and holds it in a tender embrace, saying: "Now you know that we are inseparable." The soul looks down and sees its own form no longer as a body of light, but as a body fully composed of Love.

And then, hand in hand, the two, who are one, stroll away through the radiance of Paradise, joyously praising the All-Merciful.

The guide then leads the soul to a vast window at the border of Paradise. From here the soul can look out on Allah's creation, both in its cosmic sweep, and in its intimate, living detail. Gazing at this awesome display, the soul suddenly feels intense nostalgia.

"Beloved guide. Can one ever return to the created universe from Paradise?"

Once more, smiling gently, the guide replies: "There is no separate realm which you call creation."

Through the spiritual potency of the words themselves, the soul perceives immediately that this is not a window, but a vast, spherical mirror that surrounds Paradise on all sides. When the elements of Paradise are reflected in the immense curvature of this mirror, they appear as the elements of creation. The flowing streams of Paradise, when reflected, appear as the streams of all sentient life. When the dancing maidens of Paradise are reflected, they appear as the life-bearing planets. When the dervishes of Paradise are reflected, they appear as the precious, human souls. The entire universe is simply the reflection of a dream.

While contemplating this marvelous correspondence of creation and Paradise, the soul catches sight of its own earthly form, standing in a house on a Spring morning, gazing across a river. The soul reports:

"Beloved guide: "I have a vivid sensation of being in two places at once."

"Again smiling, the guide replies: "When you look at your face in a mirror, do you really imagine that you are in two places at once? Are you not always where your original form is?"

Once again, the words of the guide carry initiatory power, and the soul, when it looks back to catch another glimpse of its earthly form, perceives all creation as a reflection of its own face.

Overwhelmed by this realization, the soul turns to its guide, only to see all of Paradise, and even the beloved guide himself, as a reflection of its own face. Nothing disappears. All being, in brilliant detail, is simply perceived as one face.

Then a voice is heard, emanating from the rivers and gardens and dervishes of Paradise, and emanating as well from all the crystal clear facets of creation. Do you accept this pure Love, in all its forms, as Allah's embrace? And not simply this soul, but all souls, who are essentially one, answer simultaneously, "Yes!"

That was from a dream I had a few years ago due to my friendship with Sheikh Muzafer Effendi, the leader of a dervish order from Istanbul. And it is part of an introduction to a manuscript I am working on now on the Holy Koran. Here are a few more offerings from this work in progress, around some more of the *suras* of the Holy Koran:

My beloved Mohammed.
This is the profoundly living book of Truth,
clear from all doubts,
which guides those whose lives are turned completely
to Allah, the source of Love,
and who experience the invisible divine Presence everywhere.

This living Koran guides those who plunge whole-heartedly
into the prayers of Islam,
and who share freely whatever abundance
the ever-present source now speaking has provided them.

This Holy Koran guides those who accept with reverence
the divine words which have been transmitted through you,
beloved Mohammed, and the words of Truth sent
from this ultimate Source through all prophets before you.

This Holy Koran guides those
who experience spontaneous faith
that after the sleep of death they will awaken
into the radiance of Allah, or Paradise.
These are the truly human beings who are receiving
the direct guidance of Allah, and these are the ones who,
on every level, become fruitful.

As for those who suffer from the cancer of negation,
those who deny the very ground of their own being,
it makes no real difference whether you teach them or not,
Beloved Mohammed,
for they simply cannot affirm the Source of being.
To protect them from becoming consumed
by their own negativity,
Allah has sealed their secret heart and their spiritual hearing,
and has covered their inner eyes with a veil.
When they die, Divine Radiance will be
a terrible purification for them.

There is but one ultimate Source of love and power,
in Arabic called Allah, the profoundly living one,
the Life outside of time that never diminishes.

This One never sleeps, nor does
Allah ever close the eyes of His all-embracing Awareness.
To this one belongs the emanation of planetary existence,
and the seven higher planes of being,
just as all rays of sunlight belong to the sun.

Lex Hixon (Nur al-Jerrahi) received his Ph.D. in World Religions from Columbia University in 1976. He then became an adept practitioner of several of the world's sacred traditions. From 1971 to 1984 he conducted a weekly radio show in New York City called "In The Spirit," interviewing spiritual teachers from around the world. An enlightened spiritual teacher, he guided many souls along their chosen path. Among his books are *Great Swan, Mother of the Universe, Heart of the Koran, Atom from the Sun of Knowledge, Mother of the Buddhas,* and *Living Buddha Zen.* For more information inquire at: nurashkijerrahi.org & srv.org

Swami Sunirmalananda

THE REALITY OF PEACE
Mentally Dissolving the False Ideas of War and Violence

Is darkness real or light real? What is the natural state of the world? Which part of the 24 hours, night or day, is the actual thing? If my question is confusing, consider this example. Many countries have daylight saving time. Every six months, you are told to turn your clocks either backwards or forwards. Until yesterday you thought it was 11 a.m. now. But from today, due to your own turning the clock, it becomes 10 a.m. now. And you believe it completely. Which one was real? 11 a.m. or 10 a.m.?

Is peace real or war? Is violence real or nonviolence? The unwritten rule of the universe is, whatever is real or permanent will remain, and whatever is superimposed will go. That which is born will have to die. If peace is real it will have to remain, and the superimposed conflict and violence will have to go. If otherwise, all efforts to stabilize peace as a permanent quality of the world will be in vain.

Thus, even as the much-desired peace is evading humanity, we may try to find out the reasons for restlessness and violence. Peace and nonviolence are essential. We have been talking all along about peace and nonviolence. At the same time, we have been witnessing wars and violence constantly. This is the irony of life. History is witness to humanity's violation of its own desire for peace time and again. Every war tires out the soul. After every war there comes the declaration that we have had enough. Yet, a new war breaks out somewhere, soon. This is the mystery of life. Why does this happen? Why are there wars and violent behavior patterns in the world?

Perhaps peace is just a superimposition. Maybe we are basically warmongers and violence-lovers. Is this possible? No, this is not possible. Our nature is not warmongering. As children or as elders, we can't be warmongers due to the nature of the body. It is only during youth that violence and war may attract us. Even that applies to some particular mindsets only, since not everyone is interested in war. Further, wars generally get triggered not due to mass activity, but due to someone or some body of people becoming greedy, ambitious, and violent. The masses are helplessly herded into the war-world, and to its consequences.

So war is not a natural state for human beings, for the simple reason that it doesn't bring universal happiness. Our natural tendency is to undertake those tasks which yield pleasure and happiness. If humans were naturally inclined to war and violence, they wouldn't be contemplating an end of war and running to their wives and children. Thus the battlefield is not the natural recreation-place of human beings. War is not the natural state of life also, because it acts more like a disease than a pastime, more like a discordant note than a symphony, and more like a malfunction than a smooth running of things.

If violence is not our natural state, why do wars happen and why does violence continue? Is it due to the instinct of survival? Let's imagine that human nature is, like that of all life, one of competition and struggle for survival. Let's imagine, then, that wars are the result of the desire for survival. The survival of the fittest is the rule, say the scientists, that governs all life. So can we credit war and violence to our basic instinct at survival? No, this is not possible. Nature has plenty, and it can provide for all living creatures. It is true that humans, when in increased numbers, tend to migrate, create unrest, look for food, etc. But this problem can be answered in a different way than by wars.

Humans are islands and society is a secondary need. Even though the survival of the fittest is the scientific law, survival is just the basic instinct and the struggle for survival is not so apparent in humans. Competition, the desire to dominate, the ambition to lead the herd, the urge to manifest power — though these are apparent, they are secondary, and let's remember that these secondary instincts, too, are neither all-time instincts nor universal. Society is needed for survival, for basic necessities, for family.

So far so good. The other drives, like dominance over others, come subsequently. That is, once I have food and shelter and clothing, I begin to look for other sources of enjoyment. I shall now wish to show my strength, conquer neighbors, etc. However, the hidden but evident nature of human beings is to follow a leader. So wars have not been fought by the masses, but by some emperor or king who had no problems with survival and who had the next generation of drives acting upon him. That is, once my stomach is full I look for other things, depending on my inclinations. Thus, the survival of the fittest is not the cause of war and violence, especially in societies where laws and moral codes have been set. There, desire is also present to help others survive. That makes us human.

Thus, if peace is not a superimposition on war, and the survival instinct is not the driving force for violence, what is? Can we say humans are by nature destroyers? Perhaps we human beings are the cancer cells of the earth. Wherever the human being goes, there forests recede, animals die, pollution ensues, natural resources are used up, environment weeps. We use up the much-needed resources of the earth, like air, water, etc. We destroy the earth.

So basically, we are cancerous. Could this be the reason why peace and nonviolence remain distant dreams? It's as if human beings, like cancer cells in the body, eat up the earth slowly. Even in so-called peaceful times, this process of our spreading of this type of cancer on the earth continues. And when the cancer seems to spread farther and farther, nature takes to chemotherapy. That is, tsunami, floods, earthquakes, epidemics, etc result. Human growth is contained. The earth breathes a sigh of relief. This is seconded by scientists who say that without human intervention, nature can quickly multiply and remain green, fresh, and unpolluted. A direct result of this cancerous occupation of the planet is violence and war. Thus, could human beings be the cancer of the earth and so there is war and violence?

No, this is not possible either. However loud scholars and scientists shout about the degradation of nature all around, and however loud young and instigated speakers recite mugged up speeches to promote the new religion called environmentalism, environment is what it is. The reason why nature gets polluted, the reason why carbon increase happens, the reason why nature becomes pale and dead, the reason why water gets polluted, is different. You make tons and tons and tons of steel to sell and to use, you make countless things in abundance and destroy nature, and then you blame the poor little man by telling him that his cart is causing carbon emission? No doubt all are concerned about nature and pollution, and no doubt many are asking the same question: Is there the true and sincere desire to contain pollution? So it is once again the story of the king wanting war and herding the masses towards it. This is the best argument.

Additionally, despite the fact that humans can and are polluting nature, two-thirds of the earth is water, and we are not the only inhabitants of the earth. Nature knows balance. It understands that all — humans, fishes, elephants, ants, volcanoes — are necessary. So to think that humans are like cancer cells of the earth is reading only one little chapter of the huge novel.

Once upon a time, there was a complaint that the wood of some forest in some country couldn't be sold. The reason was that woodpeckers were boring holes in the trees, and that the wood had virtually become useless. So, the local government ordered the killing of woodpeckers. "Shoot them dead." Gone. The next year, instead of having great wood, business people saw that there was no forest at all. What happened was interesting. Beetles saw that their enemies, the woodpeckers, had been killed, so they enjoyed absolute freedom and destroyed the whole forest. Whom will you now call the cancer of nature? Woodpeckers are needed, and so are beetles. Nature is a perfect balance of all forms of life.

Let's not be too self-critical. Let's not think that we are a curse on nature. We fit into this plan perfectly, unless, of course, we overdo and overburden nature, and this is true not only of we humans, but also of animals and mountains — like Mount Vesuvius. Not to overburden nature means not to be greedy and dominating. As they say, you are not the last user. Not to be greedy is possible if we, like the rest of nature, understand that we must use things judiciously, and that nature gives in abundance. Live and let live. When this happens, we become beneficial bacteria of the earth.

So humans alone are not to blame. In this way, till now, we have assumed that human nature causes wars and have rejected that, we have assumed that human beings are cancerous to the earth and have rejected that. What else could be the reason for war and violence? Let's look at the whole thing in a different way. Whether it is the philosopher or the scientist, all are of one voice that this world, this solid world which we experience, is not absolute or real.

To explain, the earth and external nature, according to some, is inert, or is just an objective mass. It is our mind that puts life and color to it. Edmund Husserl has said that the outer world is just a suggestion. It is the inner consciousness that makes things up. The Buddhists say almost the same thing. All the four schools [*Sautrantika, Vaibhasika, Yogachara* and *Madhyamika*] declare that everything is momentary, though they have differences of opinion about how far external objects are real. They all, however, say that it is the mind that is seeing bitterness or sweetness in objects.

And this is also the argument of Vedanta. While the dualists say that you see what your mind wishes to see, the *Advaitins* say that your seeing is relative. The Dualists say that your mind is the central thing. This is because, initially, you see the world as filled with joy and sorrow. But when you become a devotee of God you think that the world is His sport. Then everything becomes sweet for you. So it is you who colors the world. The Advaitins say that you can think whatever you want about a hologram. Yes, the universe is a hologram. Shankaracharya was the first person in recent times to declare that everything is relative. He said that nothing is absolute. Time is relative, space and causation, too, are relative.

Thus, shall we say our outlook itself is wrong? That is, are we making too much of this violence and war? Are we seeing war and violence? Let's give an example.

There is something lying on the ground. Did you see a snake in that thing? That is perfectly sensible. Did you say that you were confused, and it was just a piece of rope after all? That too, says Shankara, is perfectly sensible. When you saw the snake, it was sensible. When you saw the rope, that too was sensible. How can both be possible? If you ask him as to how both things can be possible simultaneously, he will ask this counter question: *"Who said it was simultaneous? You saw a snake and then you saw a piece of rope. All I said was, both your conclusions are okay."* How can that be possible? It can be possible, and this strange thing is called *anirvachanîya khyâti*. If you say that seeing the snake or something lying on the floor was an error, then seeing the rope also is an error, in the absolute sense. One error was for a moment, another error just lasted a longer time. That is all.

In Vedantic language, *khyâti* means error, say, an error of judgement [in Patanjala and Buddhism, *khyati* also means clarity/discernment]. You have perfect vision, you are awake and sensible, but yet you see certain things sometimes, which are not there. For instance, you saw your friend in the supermarket, or you thought you saw him, when he was elsewhere. You see something which was not there, and then, perhaps due to proper light and awareness, you see something else. Each school gives a different name and explanation to this strange phenomenon. Shankara calls it *anirvachaniya*, inexplicable. It is just inexplicable. And we are seeing things all around us all the time: tables, chairs, houses, cars. Ask a physicist what it is all about. He will say, "matter is not matter." You see something on the ground, you are scared that it is a snake, and then you laugh when it is just a rope. All this can happen. That is, both the snake and the rope are true, at those particular moments.

This *anirvachaniya khyati*, or inexplicable error of perception, is possible, says Shankara, because everything is relative. Time, space, causation — all are relative. Nothing is absolute or real. If you argue that what you are seeing now, this world, is just as it is, being neither good nor bad? No, this too is not possible, unfortunately, for the simple reason that the external, objective universe is real, relatively or essentially is another matter, so long as we see it and experience it. It is different when you become illumined. But till then, it is all real. Shankara, even though explaining the phenomena, did not deny phenomena. He gave equal importance to all the states of existence. It is wrong to imagine that Shankaracharya denied the universe. So, there is this objective universe, there is this objective war, and there is violence and all these things are happening. We are not imagining or dreaming these things. True, in the absolute sense nothing is real. But relatively, all this is happening. It is like this.

Swami Vivekananda was walking along the desert. At a distance he saw that a beautiful lake, with trees and bushes, was walking along too. He realized quickly that it was a mirage and laughed. The mirage continued to be there, but he knew. So when we know this is not absolute, we change. Thus, something more is needed to know the how and why of war and violence.

First, let us forget the question as to which one of the two —

> "....this world is called the dualistic world. It is *karma-bhumi*, and here, light and darkness, sorrow and happiness, good and bad, both are there all the time. This is the nature of the world. So peace is there and there is war, violence is there and there is nonviolence. However, if we look at things horizontally, we shall see this duality. If we look from a different perspective, it will be different. So what is the idea? We should change. We should change our locus. We should change the way we look, we should change ourselves."

solid and real, Shankara again argues that this also is relative. And the physicist is saying repeatedly that there is nothing solid, and it is all just imaginary matter.

Nowadays, adding lunacy to confusion, there is one more problem; or, shall we say, confusion is much more realistic. When you go to see a zoo created by Augmented Reality, you will be scared to death to see a lion walking around you, or surprised to see a penguin splashing water on your chair. But that is all gone the next moment. Nothing is there. Now this is going to become the usual thing of the future world. They called IoT, the Internet of Things. When this Augmented Reality will soon become a net and a natural net, you will be living inside another dream world and you will get adjusted to that. Your dreams when you sleep are one reality, your world around when you are awake is another reality, and the internet of things that brings you another world is yet another reality. All depends on how much you believe in each of them. And to escape from these nets you need something more. You should stand on something else to view all these miracles of science and nature objectively.

From this angle, then, what about war and violence? Is it a projection of your mind? Are you just imagining terrible wars and violence and getting scared? Is the objective, inert world darkness and light — is real. In the relative universe, both are real. Let us forget the question as to which of the two, war or peace, is the essential thing. In the relative world, both are real. Therefore is this world called the dualistic world. It is *karma-bhumi*, and here, light and darkness, sorrow and happiness, good and bad — both are there all the time. This is the nature of the world. So peace is there and there is war, violence is there and there is nonviolence. However, if we look at things horizontally, we shall see this duality. If we look from a different perspective, it will be different. So what is the idea? We should change. We should change our locus. We should change the way we look, we should change ourselves.

We said that the instinct of survival leads to competition, war, and violence. And we said that this is the basic instinct, this desire to survive. However, humans have the capability to look at this entire problem from a different perspective. And that is the true perspective. That is, you need not have to struggle here for survival. You can have a higher source of living. For this, once again we need a higher pedestal, a higher perspective. Let us understand why we have to survive here, why we are here, and why we suffer here. The why is more important than fighting for survival. When we understand the reason behind our

> "Why is peace the ideal and not war? This is because our internal, essential nature IS peace. Multiplicity rests on unity and oneness. And That oneness is the *Atman*."

coming, our struggles, and our efforts, we shall do something about it all, rather than worrying about killing others to eat. Why is very important. What is that why? It is *karma*. *Karma* is the central issue for our coming to the earth, for our living here and suffering. We can take care of our *karma*, and thus the very question of "struggle for survival" can be eliminated. There is no struggle anymore, but only peace.

Additionally, we need not be a cancer of the earth, but beneficial bacteria instead. All we need to do is to plant a few more trees, for instance, or do things which affect our nature positively. These things can be done. Further, we can be a blessing to the earth. For this, again, we need a higher pedestal to stand upon.

This leads us to the final point. We have mentioned philosophers who say that it is our mind that is important. However, we need not worry about how our minds react to external nature. We can do something about this. What is it? We must look beyond. If we think we are just the passing phenomena, then we are only the body. If we think we are witnesses of the passing phenomena, we are the mind. But if we think that we are the base, the foundation, the everything of the everything, then we see we are the Self, the infinite, peaceful, eternal, *Atman*. Our outlook of the world will change if our outlook of ourselves changes. When we think we are the infinite and birthless Self, we know that war and violence and so on are all relative and superficial things of the external world.

"How can I be healthy, doctor?" asked a frail, young man. "Exercise, my son," replied the doctor. Well, the frail mind needs exercise too, and that exercise is meditation. Doing this is enough to learn in order to call a spade a spade, to see things in a clear light.

Will the world be absolutely peaceful and nonviolent ever? Perhaps it cannot be. We must accept the fact. But what is the harm in trying? Though this world is dualistic, why not make it "monistic," a world of peace and nonviolence? At least can there be maximum peace and very little violence and war? Yes, that is possible, especially now, when there is the powerful social media which connect all humans, and which carries messages faster. Through social media we can spread awareness that war is a waste, violence is a waste, and peace is the solution to all problems. Further, we can tell people who know this that war is only a disease, and peace and health is the natural state.

Will everyone listen to us? It depends, but many will. And finally, it all filters down to the essential "me." I must become peaceful internally. Whatever the irritant outside, whatever the external situation outside, I should be peaceful within. The power of good is more than the power of evil. If an evil man can spread violence, a peaceful man can spread peace more readily. This is the eternal law.

So the peaceful person, who has found inner peace through contemplation and prayer, will be a great help. These little lamps of peace and nonviolence in different parts of the earth, working silently towards peace, can bring about a great change. More than anything else, the ideals should be peace and nonviolence, and not war and violence. This truth — that disease is not natural but health, war is not natural but peace — should become the ideal, irrespective of what fundamentalist scriptures teach. This lesson, that war isn't the ideal, but rather peace, should be pumped through media.

Why is peace the ideal and not war? This is because our internal, essential nature IS peace. Multiplicity rests on unity and oneness. And That oneness is the *Atman*.

We have said that war and peace, violence and nonviolence, and such other dualities are natural for the external world. Light, Peace, Love, and Nonviolence are the natural, essential, existential states of the inner world. That inner world is one of bliss, *Ananda*. In the abiding internal world, is there no competition, struggle for survival, etc? No, there isn't any. There cannot be any, for the simple reason that the *Atman* is full, is everything, and has no competition. *"He is all and everything, I am He."* We are that one. Venturing inwards, we tap the source of peace. Thus, peace and nonviolence shall become the ideals of the external universe also. So, while seeking external peace and nonviolence, we are advised to find it within, as well.

Finally, what is the difference between the external and the internal? Can we bridge both? Yes. The difference between the internal and the external is all superficial. There is One infinite existence. This we divide as subject and object, this and that, but That One is all peace and love.

Swami Sunirmalananda is a sannyasin of the Ramakrishna Order, and the monk in-charge of the Vedanta Society of Holland. He is Swami Bhuteshanandaji's disciple. The Swami had the privilege of serving his guru for a decade before serving the Ramakrishna Order's centers in Brasil and Geneva.

ADVAITA VEDANTA AND GURU-BHAKTI
The Ideal and the Inspiration

On August 3rd, 1986, Swami Aseshanandaji gave this talk to the Vedantists at the Vedanta Society of Portland who had gathered to celebrate Swami Ramakrishnananda's auspicious birthday celebration.

Swami Vivekananda, Swami Brahmananda, Swami Turiyananda, and other direct disciples of Sri Ramakrishna stand for a philosophy that is universal, that is nondogmatic, which is to forge a unity between the East and the West, between religion and religion, between science and religion. This is a very difficult task they do, for the swamis of this Order to speak to Christian nations in the West.

Christianity has tremendous power in the form of money, in the form of democracy, in the form of scientific investigation, and in the form of building an affluent society which is a kind of wonder to all those who think in terms of basic values of life. Therefore, many Eastern people have come to the West, especially to America. Why have they come? Really, it is to build a bridge of understanding. But how far have they been able to build that bridge is very difficult for me to say at present.

America, like Japan, thinks in terms of scientific achievement, a properous society, and especially freedom of women. However, it is very difficult to work in the spirit of renunciation, because Protestant countries follow the *bhogamarga*, and in order to follow that path of enjoyment one must seek power, wealth, and popularity.

So here I am, speaking more to those people who will think in terms of values that are eternal, not transitory. In a letter from Ramakrishnananda to Paramananda, that when I read it gave me a tremendous enthusiasm, he said that to represent Sri Ramakrishna one should practice lifelong *brahmacharya*. You may get eloquence, money, and many disciples and devotees, but those things are not important in the eyes of Sri Ramakrishna. Living a pure life, living an unsullied life, untainted life, an uncontaminated life — this is what is important to begin. Therefore, if any swami of the Ramakrishna Order is to speak to the West, he will do so from the platform of unbroken brahmacharya so that the conviction of his direct experience will shine through.

And this is where I would bring in *Guru-bhakti*. This was the permanent feature in Swami Ramakrishnananda's life. In the case of Swami Vivekananda, he was the *rishi*, the great seer. It is a seer of that incomparable stature that will introduce *Advaita Vedanta* to the world in such an age as this. That must remain as the key for all of the problems of life, as well as the problem of death. Only on two occasions did Swami Vivekananda speak about Sri Ramakrishna in the West, both under the caption of "my Master." He was silent about his *guru*, but he was very eloquent about *Advaita Vedanta*.

The West forms a dualistic set of civilizations. There is dualism, first, about subject and object. This was given by the Greek philosophers. Therefore, after the Renaissance, faith played the greatest part, to be understood only by the faithful through the lens of what is practical. Then, science declared that reason will be the cure for all the problems facing the individual in his life, and in social life as well. So, you will find, if you inspect deeper, there is fundamental dualism between man and the universe from the standpoint of scientific achievement of Western man, and there is also dualism between man and God, creature and Creator. This has come from the Judaic faith. And the third type of dualism comes from the middle-eastern countries around the concepts of good and evil.

And so, these countries, in present times, are saturated and suffused by the philosophy of dualism, a standing example of which you find today in South Africa [still in apartheid]. Simply sending a black diplomat from America will not solve the problem unless man begins to think in terms of the universal nature of all men. Otherwise leaders think that the cause of all problems is a matter of pigmentation. For the white person, that is the reason that they walk and lie on the beach. [laughter]

So, this color problem is a very difficult problem for Western man to solve. Western Jews are white, you see, but I have seen, in Malabar, that the Jews there have brown colored skin. I admire the attempt at emancipation of negroes and other unjustly treated groups. But that is not my field. My field is the field of individual spiritual realization, and one can never realize God unless one lives a pure life and penetrates through all forms of persistent dualism of this world. Teach your children from the cradle to the grave to live a life directed towards the Ultimate Reality. Never teach them to "have fun," but rather to transcend good and evil. In order that they accomplish this they must be morally strong, ethically pure, and spiritually integrated.

So, when I think of Swami Ramakrishnananda, I think of all his lectures. They were all grounded in *Advaita* philosophy, but at the same time they were combined with devotion to the *guru*, a combination which every monk of the Ramakrishna Order will have to accept, have to understand, and will have to realize in order to preach *Advaita* in the West. It must be based in knowledge of the divinity of mankind, as Swami Vivekananda has declared. In this task it would have been better if the expression, "Original Sin," had never been used. It is this sin-obsessed Christianity that has grown out of the teachings of Saint Augustine, and given by Paul into its fold.

Accordingly, then, there is a huge amount of difference between the Indian concept of *Avatar* and the Western one. In the latter case, the *Avatar* comes as a redeemer, but in India the *Avatar* comes to reinforce the truth of the divinity of man, the harmony of religions, and realization based upon the personal experience of God in a transcendental state of Consciousness.

And it here that we find that it is Advaita alone which will solve the problems of man, whether in the East or in the West. In the Americas Swamiji spoke about pure Vedanta; in the East he spoke about practical Vedanta. In practical Vedanta, every man is a manifestation of the Divine Spirit whom we will love, worship, as well as adore — in our shrines, in our churches, in our synagogues, and in our temples. In order to communicate the truth of nonduality from India, when the Hindus come here they must be able to represent Hinduism at its best. Unfortunately, as in other religions as well, some there are who will try to turn it into a business, for a personal profit. The Ideal, here, should not be allowed to become westernized.

Recently, I was distressed to hear of the fighting between the Hindus and the Sikhs. But now they have become good friends again. That is the right attitude. The Hindus ought to be able to be friends not only with the Sikhs, but even with the Canadians up in Canada [laughter]....and with the Americans in the United States. For, you see, mankind is known by his actions. Our action must stem from a heart which is pure, which brooks no evil. That is what Holy Mother taught us. *"My child, if you want peace of mind, don't see any evil."* If there is any evil in your heart, remove it, like a beam or a mote of dust in the eye.

When I was last in India, I lived in Benares for three years. I used to go to the Visvanath temple every day, and carry Ganges water to Siva there. There is the Hindu belief, you see, that if

ideal parents who are Vedantists should be such an example to their children, that the children will learn more from those parents than they will from the leaders of the church. It is the home that will give strength, power, nobility and grandeur to the family.

But I am talking, as well, to those who have gone from the family home, to the homeless stage of life. That life I connect to Jesus, to Buddha, to Sri Ramakrishna, and to their ecstatic disciples. Therefore, the Protestant religion has a drawback. It does not allow a man or a woman to renounce the world and embrace a monastic life. It is like a bird with one wing. To renounce the world in Christianity one would have to become a Catholic, due to this drawback in Protestantism. Again, however, each is good in its own place; I would not want to make any final comparison. I would only insist, that to be a teacher of religion one must renounce the world. There should not be any "axe to grind," as they say. They are not here to please husband, wife, or children; they will try to please God.

And in order to please God there must be freedom. Freedom, with regards to living a contemplative life. Such a one will not go about always thinking of doing good to the world, for the moment one has that thought, one is suddenly going about not doing good at all, but hampering the higher good. You can never do good to any person until you have done the highest

> "....in Benares, I went to see Swami Turiyananda. He gave me a strong desire to renounce the world. Americans are householders. I tell you, how much time do you spend as husbands to please your wives? And wives to please your husbands? How much time? With even half of that time, if you used that same energy, you would realize God."

you go and die in Benares you will attain liberation. And so I saw old ladies going there after living a life of worldliness. They had become tired of life. But living in Benares, I saw them trying to prolong their lives. [laughter] They wanted to prolong their lives for the sake of grandsons getting married in Kolkata [laughter] You see, then, Lord Siva does not grant liberation so soon.

But I went to Benares not only to see Siva, but to see illumined souls. You here in this country may love and seek sights and sounds, children, presidents, and the like, but we Hindus love illumined souls.

So there, in Benares, I went to see Swami Turiyananda. He gave me a strong desire to renounce the world. Americans are householders. I tell you, how much time do you spend as husbands to please your wives? And wives to please your husbands? How much time? With even half of that time, if you used that same energy, you would realize God. And also, spend some of that time to try and raise your children to a higher level of consciousness.

So a great problem with America, you see, is to try to satisfy the family with pleasures. Those devotees who have come here, to the Vedanta center, are also householders, and I pray God speed your efforts to become an ideal householder. The

good to yourself. It reminds me of a certain person......

During the last war, our high school building was given to what was called "Air Raid Station." This was in Madras when I was an older student. The leader was called the "warden." He would take us to the shelter room when the Japanese bombers were circling over Madras and Hardwar. Sandbags were strewn around there, you see. But there was no safety against a direct hit, falling from straight above.

At five o'clock, early in the morning, the siren went off and we were told to make our way to the shelter. I was in my room. And I said to myself, "Who can kill me if my time has not come?" So I stayed. Then the principle came and said, "If you do not go to the shelter, the younger boys will not go, since you are their teacher." So I went.

In the shelter, Ramanuja, the secretary, told me to recite the *Gita* for the boys, to give courage and strength. That helped us through the trial, with bombs bursting all around. Then the principle came and told us that the warden who was in charge had had a nervous breakdown. He used to come and tell us, "Don't be nervous. [laughter] When the siren goes off, just go to the shelter and be quiet." But he himself fainted.

Dualistic religion also says the same. It tells us not to be afraid. But when trials come, it fails. It becomes a mockery. But

Sri Ramakrishna has come to make religion pure. Edifying. Uplifting. And also to make religion universal. The intricate message of Sri Ramakrishna will make religion all-encompassing for the highest good of all living beings. In addition, it will give undaunted fearlessness that will face off with any problem that will come in this pilgrimage of life.

So here, I have to tell the Western people, especially the scientists, that you have made Nature infinite and man finite. This is a travesty of Truth. In the Vedanta, as preached by Sri Ramakrishna, as preached by Swami Vivekananda, as preached by Swami Turiyananda, and as preached by Swami Ramakrishnananda, Nature is finite and man is infinite. They are not just Tom, Dick, and Harry, but illumined souls. [laughter] Additionally, you need a scripture. Bible is a scripture, no doubt, but it has not been interpreted in a nondualistic sense. The great Theologians of the West have rendered Christ's words in a dualistic way.

Christ's main teaching was *"I and my Father are one."* He said to the Samarian woman, *"God is not in the hills of Samaria that the Samaritan people worship, God is not in the temples of Jerusalem that the Jews worship; God is Spirit. They who will worship God will worship in Spirit."* So, when you worship God in Spirit and in Truth you must necessarily think that your self is potentially divine, to be potentially perfect, to be potentially illumined, or potentially moral.

And that is why, regarding scripture, I will have to introduce into your consciousness the message of the Upanisads. Its great message is *Tat Tvam Asi* — Thou Art That. Although Ramanuja interprets this as being that you belong to God, that is because he thinks of man's nature being finite. But not Shankara. Your real nature, *Atman*, is Infinite. On account of ignorance you are thinking yourself to be finite. True religion is nothing but dehypnotization. You have hypnotized yourself into thinking that you were born, and that some day you will die. And perhaps if you are a particularly faithful devotee of a religion that you will go to heaven.

But Vedanta tells you that birth is illusory, death is illusory, and going to heaven, also illusory. So try and be a *jivanmukta*. That is a living liberated soul. If you have climbed Mt. Everest, you can say so, and then take others there. But if you have not even understood the meaning of Christ's words, then you must keep silent in the presence of a *jivanmukta*. Further, I would make a distinction between Christ and "Churchianity." The church has taken the place of true religion. Therefore it is bound to be what you call dogmatic.

You have sent missionaries to different parts of the world. What right have you to do that? Because you have power? Because you have the atom bomb? And you have demonstrated that power at Nagasaki and Hiroshima. But that is not Christ's religion. That is "vanity of vanities." He who draws the sword will pay through the sword. Instead, you are to convert your swords into plowshares. For the only way you can truly practice real religion is through spiritual power, not worldly power, through nonviolence, not through violence.

And that is the reason that I say, India, with all your faults — I have not visited you since I came to this country in 1947 — but with all your faults I love you still, because you have produced a great man like Sri Ramakrishna and a great woman like Holy Mother. They have charmed my eyes, dazzled my inner vision, and given me the strength to speak to the American people in this way.

So now, I have to bring it down a little [laughter]. Just try to live religion. Religion cannot be preached only; it cannot be propagated through your news media. Religion can also not be forced on other people. Religion must be lived. Ty to be an exemplar of religion. That means try to be an illumined soul. That kind of soul was called in the *Upanisadic* days a *guru*.

Today, some Eastern men have come here and given a false connotation of the word *guru*. They write books about themselves lauding their own egos. If any of these Hindu men think that to be a *guru* is to drive around in a Rolls-Royce car, or a Cadillac car, or a Lincoln Imperial, or a Mercedes car, that is not the test of a real *guru*. His senses must be under control, his energy must be pure, and he must have controlled his own mind. He must not care about cars, but about freeing souls. This is the way.

The energy we get from food, it is to be stored up and become converted into *ojas*. We do not create energy, we only change it. As heat is converted into light, light is changed into electricity, and electricity is changed into radiation, in the same way biological energy can be converted into spiritual energy through the path of renunciation, through the path of self-control, through the path of self-enlightenment. Sri Ramakrishna stressed that idea. It is a conservation of spiritual energy. It is the concentrated mind that will give you this special energy.

Your William James accepted that. The mind's rays, he said, are like the rays of the sun. They are all diffused. But with a lens you can focus your energy. That is called *tapas*. If you concentrate the mind on matter you become an object, but if you concentrate the mind on God you become an illumined soul — a real *guru*; a dispeller of darkness.

Swami Vivekananda — he finished the Encyclopedia Britannica, and also kept all of it with his power of retention. If you can master concentration of mind you will be able to retain it, for a long, long time. In this regard, a few words that Swami Saradananda spoke to me will remain with me all through my life. What did he say? At Durga Puja one night, he said to me: "Do not depend upon anybody. Stand on your own feet. Try to live the life of the Spirit and Sri Ramakrishna will be the source of your strength, and the fountainhead of your realization." He also told me that night to be not like the creeper that depends on the tree, but to make my own decisions. Thus, though I may live in America, my mind remains with the great souls I have met and learned from in India. They have lent me the Inspiration to realize the Ideal.

Swami Aseshananda, a direct disciple of Sri Sarada Devi, Sri Ramakrishna's wife and spiritual consort, was the Spiritual Minister of the Vedanta Society of Portland for over forty years. He also received holy company with some of the direct disciples of the Great Master. He is the author of *Glimpses of a Great Soul*, on the life and teachings of Swami Saradananda.

Spiritual Tools for Peace of Mind

Ask almost anyone these days, "how are you?", and one is likely to receive an answer detailing in various ways how they are under stress. Stress, anxiety, worry, the burden of responsibility, fear for survival, making deadlines – all these seem uppermost in the minds of those around us. But all the stress that we experience hinges on certain assumptions about ourselves and the world and a lack of concentration, manifesting as habitual distraction. Adept spiritual practitioners get rid of these naturally over time through inner practices combined with contemplation and meditation. They achieve abiding peace and compassionate detachment. We can too.

The essential false assumption made with regard to oneself, in *yogic* language, is *"taking the Seer to be the seen."* This confusion is a fundamental concern of the Yoga system presented by Patanjali, and its practices are meant to aid us in separating the two so that *samadhi* is possible. The seer cannot be the seen. This is like saying "I am my car." Laughable and too obvious, yes, but people do this by unhesitatingly assuming "I am my body." And that is just the beginning.

Returning to the issue of experiencing stress and anxiety, people often deal with it in at least two basic ways. One is to find a pleasurable activity to get absorbed in, and the other is simply going to sleep. The deficiency of both of these is that they are temporary fixes. One will eventually wake up and return to these stressful situations, and any pleasurable activity comes to an end without solving the issue. Still, these two avenues give us a clue as to what we are really seeking. Getting absorbed in an enjoyable activity brings the mind to a place of some concentration. The less "busy" the diversion the better – like a hike in nature as opposed to scrolling through a social media app. A sense of relative peace unfolds the more one-pointed the mind becomes on its object. When one concentrates, one wave of thought subdues all the other waves of thought. In the case of sleep, the hidden secret here is that one removes all objects from the mind. A deep, dreamless sleep is rejuvenating, and from the *yogic* perspective, this is precisely because there is an absence of objects; the mind is at rest in this relative emptiness. In it, one unconsciously experiences the bliss of the Self, albeit, through the veil of nescience.

How can we translate these two temporary ways of dealing with stress into ongoing experiences? How can we achieve peaceful one-pointedness while engaged in daily life, and how can we consciously taste the bliss of the Self? Daily, ongoing spiritual practices – formal and "on the go," both – are the answer. This approach succeeds when one decides that peace of mind is essential in one's life. Taking this as one's firm mental stance, or *"manasana,"* (*manas*/mind, *asana*/posture), opens the mind to new ways of perceiving and acting.

The Seer and the Seen

The first step in a transformative spiritual practice is recognizing the distinction between the Seer and the seen, Spirit and insentient matter. [see Nectar #33, "Vedanta 101 – Spiritual Discrimination"]. This is similar to the concept of stepping back and being the "witness." But do we follow this awareness of the "witness" to its ultimate conclusion? An easy rule of thumb for this is, "if I can perceive it, then 'it' falls into the category of the seen and is insentient." Now, this runs counter to common understanding that the mind, intellect, and ego represent our sentient self. But experience shows that not only can we perceive physical, atomic objects with our senses, but we also follow the movements of our minds, inclusive of what we might call the personality, the ego, thoughts, emotions, and memories. Further, we can see how the mind shifts positions and identities when coming into contact with coworkers, teachers, parents, children, or friends. People assume that the mind, which includes all those movements, is sentient, but clearly, that which is seeing, or aware of all these movements, is a witness of another order. It is the sentient Seer. And just as the eye cannot see itself except as a reflection in a mirror or something similar, just so, the Seer cannot see Itself except as a reflection (an object) through a reflector. The mind and its components, and to a much grosser degree, the senses and body are those reflectors. If we take the analogy of the eye and the mirror and apply it to the practice of discrimination between the Seer and the seen, our experience is that we never confuse the reflected eye with the real eye. Yet, that is what we do when we take the Seer, the Witness, to be body, energy, mind, intellect, and ego.

This Seer is the subtlest of the subtle. It is unchanging. The same root "I" awareness that we have as a baby is the same as we have now, and that we have in all our activities, states of dream, and in dreamless sleep. It unites all changing experiences. Swami Vivekananda made a bold statement in one of his classes, which is relatively easy to experience for oneself. He stated,

"It is through the Self that you know anything. I see the chair; but to see the chair, I have first to perceive myself and then the chair. It is in and through the Self that the chair is perceived. It is in and through the Self that you are known to me, that the whole world is known to me; and therefore, to say this Self is unknown is sheer nonsense. Take off the Self and the whole universe vanishes."

In the Upanisads we come across the following statement:

"Meditate on the Lord as thine own Self seated in your heart, who appears to you as the Universe, and who is the true source of all beings. Perceive That as the primeval cause of the relationship between Consciousness and matter, and as the partless Divine Entity transcending the three divisions of time. Om peace, peace, peace." (*Svetashvatara Upanisad*, 6:5)

According to the Sankhya system, earth, water, fire, air, and

> "....it is false identification of the Seer with the seen that makes stress possible. If we knew ourselves at all times as the ever free, ever peaceful Seer, stress would not be possible. The system of the five sheaths is a hands-on way of recognizing these false identities and re-identifying with the Self, the Seer."

ether (*akasha*), as well as senses, mind, ego, intellect, and the Cosmic Mind, are all composed of matter – some gross, and some subtle and even causal, this latter described as a seed state, with the potential for manifestation only. They are all structures for the Sentient Self to experience phenomena, but throughout all experiences, the Seer is unaffected. It does not require phenomena for its existence. Rather, phenomena are impossible without It. This Seer is *"that one Light shining by which everything is illumined."*

The link between peace of mind and discrimination between the Seer and the seen, is that abiding peace is not possible without freedom and fearlessness. Uncovering the presence of the true Witness, the Seer, naturally reveals our inherent Freedom and our birthless, deathless nature.

Discerning False Identities – The Five Sheaths

"Forgetting your personality, try to realize your identity with God." - Sri Sarada Devi

Having understood the difference between the Seer and the seen, we can go deeper with a specific method that enables us to practice this both formally, and throughout the day. In the very first issue of Nectar is an article on *"Adhara, the System of the Five Koshas"* (available on Google Play, search for "Nectar #1"). This article gives a detailed account of the Five Sheaths covering the true Self/Seer. Returning again to the issue of stress and anxiety, it is false identification of the Seer with the seen that makes stress possible. If we knew ourselves at all times as the ever-free, ever-peaceful Seer, stress would not be possible. The system of the five sheaths is a hands-on way of recognizing these false identities and re-identifying with the Self, the Seer.

In brief, these five sheaths are conceived of as containers for all-pervasive Consciousness to express through. The following explanations are presented from the standpoint of this indivisible Consciousness, the true Seer, putting on these sheaths to experience phenomena, like a person putting on "virtual" glasses, clothing, etc., to have experiences of an alternative reality. The enlightened person never forgets who they are in this process, but the unawakened begin to forget themselves with the first layer, then believe they are these accumulating sheaths.

The sheath of bliss or ego (*anandamaya kosha*) – This is the first and most subtle sheath enwrapping the Seer. It accounts for our sense of a separate "I" – separate from other beings, nature, and God. It is our subtlest "false identity," the individual's highest witness unburdened by desire and aversion, and is the first reflection of the Seer/Atman. It is responsible for the experiences of bliss, peace, and happiness, which are only limited reflections of the absolute Bliss of the Seer. This sheath permeates and expresses through all the other sheaths.

The sheath of intellect (*vijnanamaya kosha*) – This is the next most subtle sheath. It reflects the pure Awareness and Intelligence of the Seer and conditions/objectifies it into what we call knowledge. With the sense of a separate "I" infilling it from the prior sheath, the sheath of intellect also becomes the seat of agency and ownership. It is the seat of such assertions as "this is my knowledge; these are my actions." Unrefined, this sheath is the deluding source of pride, desire for power, manipulation, and glory. When such desires are stymied, it will be dulled by dejection and the sense of worthlessness or impotence. However, when disciplined by spiritual practices that nurture wisdom, then "my knowledge" gives way to "all knowledge belongs to God," and the sense of agency gives way to offering all action and their results to God. Matured in this fashion, this sheath becomes the best reflector of the infinite and omniscient Seer/Atman and the impetus for benevolent action while embodied. This sheath permeates the following sheaths.

The sheath of dual mind (*manomaya kosha*) – This sheath represents our mental processes associated with the five senses of hearing, touching, seeing, tasting, and smelling. Desire and aversion for the objects that can be experienced with all these senses leads to a great deal of action, emotion, and reaction. The sense of agency and ownership from the prior sheaths gets intensified in the undisciplined mind that broods and obsesses over objects it has acquired or is trying to acquire. The unmatured mind, a reflection of the unlimited Seer, identifies with these thoughts and emotions and due to its connection with the senses, also looks upon the body as itself congealing, so to speak, all five sheaths and losing any sense of the true Seer. It is constantly chattering within, "This is good, bad, fun, boring. I feel happy, sad, depressed, peaceful, content, restless, bored. I want this; I don't want that. I am fat, thin, sick, healthy, wealthy, a daughter, son, spouse, parent, friend, male, female, gay, straight, worker, lawyer, evil, good, etc." This sheath infills the next.

The sheath of energy (*pranamaya kosha*) – Charged with the mental activity and atmosphere of the prior sheaths, the sheath of energy activates the body, its limbs and organs, to carry out the clear and/or conflicted commands of the sheaths of mind and intellect. This sheath of vital energy consists of 5 kinds of *prana*/force governing the body and its organs like lungs, heart, digestion, brain, etc., and also the functioning of the physical senses and the limbs. If the prior sheaths are uncontrolled, fearful, anxious, given to the passions and constantly seeking sensory indulgence, becoming over-sated or angry when thwarted, then the vital energy becomes erratic and causes havoc in the body, setting the stage for diseases of various kinds. Such havoc

> "All the sheaths will vibrate with peace, purity, and benevolence once you remain as you are, the Seer. Note that this conscious dissolving of the sheaths is what one is doing unconsciously when falling asleep, passing from the waking state full of objects, to the dream state full of mental objects, and into deep sleep where there are no objects."

includes uneven breathing, irregular heartbeat, poor digestion, problems with the brain affecting memory and judgement, to name a few very obvious indicators.

The sheath of the physical body (*annamaya kosha*) – This sheath is infilled by all previous sheaths. It consists of the five elements, or stated scientifically, it is made of matter. It only looks sentient because of the other sheaths infilling it. Similarly, the apparently sentient sheaths of mind, intellect, and ego only appear so because they reflect the Seer/*Atman*. Identification with the physical body as the Self/Seer is the cause of the mind, intellect, and ego thinking, "I am the characteristics of the body," as related above in the mental sheath. This false identification (*vivarta*) with the body is the cause of tremendous stress and anguish. However, to the extent that the Seer is in charge – only associating/using the body benignly — the body is a temple for the expression of Consciousness. This is what we see in awakened and illumined beings. They are content and at peace.

Formal Contemplation

There is a story told in SRV Associations about a magician who uses a wand to devise a complex world full of stunning natural beauty, creatures of many kinds, and human beings too. He is so fascinated by his own creation that he rushes into it, unknowingly leaving the wand behind. Distracted by activities, mesmerized by scenery, and overcome with the array of relationships unfolding, he forgets that he himself created all this and becomes trapped in cycles of happiness and sorrow and the rules of the world he created, like birth, growth, disease, decay, and death. Eventually he grows weary of all this and begins to yearn for peace. Via yearning and self-effort he eventually remembers his original role in it all, and where he left his wand. He then extricates himself from the magic projection of his own mind.

The five sheaths, presented here, is a method to be practiced by contemplation during formal sitting practice. *"Today's imagination is tomorrow's realization,"* is a Vedantic adage given early on in spiritual practice. Having heard the *dharma* teachings, one next contemplates them. This means to run them over and over in the mind with the intent to grasp a deeper level of understanding so that one can unite understanding with thought, word, and deed. From this kind of contemplation comes concentration and one-pointedness. This naturally calms the mind, which in turn balances the energy flowing into the body.

Contemplate each sheath from subtle to gross, as presented above, using the imagination to "feel" the addition of each sheath through which the pure and unlimited Seer will express, and keep that awareness uppermost with each additional sheath, all the way to the physical sheath; this is a way to practice remaining your Self, the Seer, at all levels of the psycho-physical being – *"The Eternal among all noneternal things."*

Next, contemplate in the reverse order, where each sheath is dissolved into the next most subtle sheath: body into energy, energy into mind, mind into intellect, intellect into the "separate 'I' sense," and finally dissolve all into the Seer. Use the imagination to feel your inherent, boundless Freedom and Bliss – unconditioned by the weighty objects of thought, desire, energetical forces, or physical forms. You can express through all of these again later, and with increasing identification as the buoyant Awareness whose nature is Peace and Bliss. All the sheaths will vibrate with peace, purity, and benevolence once you remain as you are, the Seer. Note that this conscious dissolving of the sheaths is what one is doing unconsciously when falling asleep, passing from the waking state full of objects, to the dream state full of mental objects, and into deep sleep where there are no objects.

Sincere practice will reveal insights and nuances that this article, and even the scriptures (which one should take recourse to), cannot relate; one must practice and experience for oneself. Further, it is necessary to take one's insights to a qualified teacher for verification; thus, one completes Vedanta's Proofs of Truth: hearing, reasoning, realizing [see box on facing page]. Formal practice of this method results in a deep clarity of the distinction between the Seer and the seen, the Self and the not-Self. This is essential for the famous Vedantic practice described as "Who am I?" (*atma vichara*); for, in order to know "who I am," one must know what one is not. The Five Sheaths is a classic and effective system for this discovery.

Who am I?

Now the practitioner is ready to take this practice "on the go." Throughout the day, monitor each "I" statement that arises in your mind, whether expressed verbally or not. Analyze which of the five sheaths it refers to and re-identify with the true Seer. The idea is that whenever one makes a statement beginning with "I," one should immediately analyze where that "I" is identified. Am I taking my body to be myself? Or the mind, or the intellect, or the ego?

In practice, especially in the beginning, one will generally find that it is difficult to distinguish easily between these sheaths. The emotions of the mind are carried by the energy sheath and felt viscerally in the organs of the body. The basic sense of agency and ownership that evolved first in the sheath of intellect are hard to tease apart from the activities of the mental sheath. The sense of "I" permeates all the sheaths. This is why we must formally contemplate each of the five and analyze our sense of

> # Vedanta's Three Proofs of Truth
>
> ◊ **Hearing the Truth (Shruti)**
>
> *Hear spiritual teachings from the lips of an illumined preceptor and also from the revealed scriptures, those scriptures expressing the nature of Reality, and the individual soul and their relationship.*
>
> ◊ **Reasoning about the Truth (Yukti)**
>
> *Contemplate, during daily formal spiritual practice, the teachings you have heard and read. Strive for full concentration in order to enter into their essential meaning. Then, apply this knowledge in daily life.*
>
> ◊ **Direct experience of the Truth (Anubhava)**
>
> *Through sincere, intense practice of the first two "proofs," one gradually transcends the intellectual frame of reference and attains "vijnana," which, according to Sri Ramakrishna is knowledge that has been realized.*
>
> All three proofs are necessary. Direct experience should accord with the revealed scriptures and the illumined preceptor, and also not contradict reason, though it will transcend reason by way of fulfilling it.

identification. As we do this, we are to remember that we are seeing each of these sheaths and mistakenly identifying ourselves accordingly. But now we recognize them as objects, and that very fact reveals the ever-present Seer so that we can place our identification in That and simply associate with the sheaths. Every "I" statement gets seen for what it is, a false identification with one of the sheaths, becoming a catalyst to remember our true identity as the Seer, the Awareness that underpins them all but is not limited to any of them. This may feel like imagination in the beginning, but persist and it will become realization. The false identities that have seemed natural over countless lifetimes take time to overcome.

Three Rudimentary Supports

There are other aids to peace of mind important for the practitioner to follow in conjunction with the above. These set one up for success and require diligence and boundary-setting. The first is to set time aside each day for spiritual practice, undisturbed by people, pets, work, and technology. Even 20 minutes is a good start. Instead of thinking, "how will I add this into my day?" ask, "how can I work my earthly life into my daily spiritual practice?" This is facilitated by regular participation with one's spiritual community. Strength and support through the challenges of maintaining a vibrant spiritual life is to be found in the company of the spiritual preceptor and fellow practitioner.

The second practical aid is to "eat when you eat." That means eating in a peaceful atmosphere and never while working, commuting, or feeling "on the go." Avoid "fast food," and cook your own meals in a meditative manner. Say a *mantra* or blessing and offer it to the inner Deity before eating. It is not a mere coincidence that the rise of fast food and eating on the run coincides with the increase of restlessness, distraction, and brooding in the minds of so many people today. And lastly, conserve energy and nurture inner peace by not taking on additional responsibilities that would make the first two practical aids impossible to maintain. In Holy Mother's, Sri Sarada Devi's, immortal words, *"Peace is essential. You need peace first and foremost."*

Annapurna Sarada is the president of SRV Associations and an assistant teacher for the sangha. She also writes on spiritual topics at Medium.com.

Live-Streaming Class Series from SRV Hawaii for 2020

▪ Successful Mantra Practice
February, 9th, 16th, & 23rd, 2020

Mantra is the sacred formula that dissolves root ignorance in the human mind. Traditionally, and most effectively, it is transmitted to the sincere disciple by the authentic teacher/guru in sacred ceremony, thereby initiating that fortunate soul into the divine mysteries of spiritual life. This entrance into Divine Life, enacted once every lifetime for as long as the soul needs, requires, or seeks said mantra-diksha, is smoothly facilitated by this powerful combination of seed words, that consist of bijams (unique words of primal origin), and a Holy Name of the Lord or Divine Mother of the Universe. Mantra, faithfully recited in the light of its intrinsic meaning, dispels ignorance and suffering, breaks down mental impressions from past lifetimes, and inspires the soul onwards towards the realization of the Atman, its own divine nature.

▪ The "Third Eye" — Kundalini's Sixth Chakra
March 8th, & 15th, 2020

Called "Jnana Chakshu" (Wisdom Eye) by Lord Krishna in the Bhagavad Gita, the "Dharma Eye" by Lord Buddha in the Dhammapada, and referred to by the saying, "If thine Eye be single thine body shalt be full of Light," by Lord Jesus in several of the Gospels, this truth-principle is mentioned by some seven different religious traditions of the world in their various and specific scriptures. In the Kundalini Yoga tradition it is termed the "Ajna Chakra," aligned with the spiritual center located symbolically at the center of the forehead. There it acts as the gateway leading from beatific vision into the realm of Nonduality Itself.

▪ Brahmapada: The Four Feet of Brahman (How Consciousness Disports Itself)
April 12th, 19th, & 26th, 2020

Generally, it could be said that Consciousness, always pure and unadulterated, appears in various shapes and forms throughout the worlds of name and form. From the nondual position, the four states of waking, dreaming, deep sleep, and Turiya are the Four Feet of Brahman, then, as Consciousness runs in and throughout them — like sweetness permeates sugar-cane juice. Additionally, the Chandogya Upanisad defines the disporting of Consciousness in more concrete terms, calling the Four Feet of Brahman speech, life-force, sight, and hearing (vak pada, prana pada, chakshu pada, and shrotra pada). There are also other profound designations for this unique and endearing term, all utilized to flesh out our understanding about Divine Reality, with form and beyond.

▪ Sri Ramachandra's Discourse of Divine Discontent
June 7th, 14th, & 21st, 2020

Very similar to Lord Buddha's young life when he left his royal father's palace in search of Enlightenment after seeing the suffering of the world for the first time, the story of Sri Ramachandra, though much earlier in time, follows along the same track. After going on pilgrimage, and departing the confines of his own royal father's Koshala kingdom, the young man saw many kinds of suffering in the peoples and places that he visited with his brother and half-brothers. Returning later to the palace, his sober demeanor, so unlike his old self, caught the attention of all and sundry in King Dasaratha's Great Hall, leading to His famous "Discourse of Divine Discontent," for the Highest Good of all present there.

▪ Prana: The Missing Link
July 12th, 19th, & 26th, 2020

When Swami Vivekananda was present in the United States in 1893, and again in the early 1900's, he made mention of the fact that the people of the West were not aware of the operations of prana, the subtle life-force that animates all of nature, as well as the senses and other motor functions. Its presence in the five elements

SRV ASSOCIATIONS
Sarada • Ramakrishna • Vivekananda
Setting the feet of humanity on the path of Universal Truth

Live-Streaming Class Series, continued

formulates our food, permeates our food, digests our food, and delivers vital energy into body, senses, and mind as well. Prana flows, it is true, even if its presence is not cognized, but once this flow is noticed, controlled, and channeled — as in the case of illumined yogis — human awareness begins to refine in quality and expand in quantity to afford the soul its first glimpses of the timeless, spaceless, birthless, deathless condition of its own divine nature. In these early and intermediary stages of spiritual awakening, prana then becomes known as psychic prana — another missing link in contemporary human thinking — revealing further the living presence of Shakti, Divine Mother power. This "link" must not go missing in us any longer.

▪Points & Principles of Brahman
September 6th, 13th, 20th, & 27th, 2020

Strewn like precious gems throughout the Upanisads of the Vedanta, and found lying like flecks of gold in India's many religious streams that flow into Her magnificent Ocean of pure, conscious Awareness, the points of Wisdom and principles of Nonduality abide, awaiting discovery and revelation. In this hot, dry, and arid world of rank materialism and gross sense gratification, these self-proclaimed axioms moisten the pages of Mother India's revealed scriptures like deep, cool water in remote desert springs. By an in-depth study of these treasures of Truth, gathered, noted, and taught by ancient rishis, ascetic yogis, world-renouncing sannyasins, and illumined preceptors, the sincere aspirant can make swift, sure, and steady progress along the often secluded and lonely Path of Enlightenment leading to the Goal of Self-realization.

▪The Path, Neti Neti; The Tool, Viveka
Separating the Wheat from the Chaff
November 8th, 15th, 22nd, & 29th, 2020

It is a known fact among the seekers and knowers of Wisdom, that in order to actually possess a spiritual life one must both practice the disciplines prescribed by preceptors, and implement that one defining purificatory tool called viveka. The especial discrimination that viveka represents means all the difference between a successful journey inwards, and a mere failed attempt at spiritual attainment. Even when the right intention is present in the seeker's mind, without viveka, the end result is either a mind filled with half-digested knowledge, or a premature departure from the noble path altogether. For, viveka separates the wheat from the chaff, speaking Biblically. Its implementation into spiritual practice amounts to taking all that is changing, alluring, distracting, and nonessential, and relegating it to a subsidiary position behind the search for Truth and Freedom — in a "get thee behind me" type of affirmation. Specifically, accomplishing the removal of all that is fleeting and misleading in life and mind outlines and indicates the main aspect of the Neti Neti path, for the soul really is "not this, not this," and needs to realize it fully so that it can know with dead certainty what it truly is — the ever-free, neverbound, ever-pure Atman. Therefore, viveka aids the aspirant seeking this fully-realized perfection via the Neti Neti path like no other tool in the arsenal of authentic religious traditions. In plain words, discrimination between the Real and the Unreal accomplishes the important mental process of "I am not this, I am not this," duly leading to the twin nondual epiphanies of Tat Tvam Asi, "I Am That," and Sarvam Khalvidam Brahma, "All of this is verily Brahman."

▪Vedanta, Theology, and Science
Comparative Views of Consciousness, Origination, Nature, & Life/Death
December 20th, & 27th, 2020

The people of the world today, living in these technical, "jet-age" times, have not only lost their hold on peace and contentment, but have also lost their connection to the ancient wisdom that is both eternal and internal. Religion is in a fallen state, having failed to bolster the faith of followers and deliver unto them the special knowledge that confers immortality upon the individual. Science, by catering to the sense-life of the society by providing objects of comfort that only weaken the physical and moral fabric of living beings, has done a further disservice. Caught between the proverbial "rock and a hard place" that Theology and Science represent, the Vedanta has now emerged, brought to us by a true World-leader in the form of Swami Vivekananda. Putting these three ideologies side by side provides for an interesting study, revealing the truth to intelligent beings who have grown weary of today's materially-oriented Science, and the aged superstitions of religion.

* **Livestream.com/Babaji Bob Kindler**

SRV Vedanta Associations — Babaji's Teaching Schedule, 2020

SRV Hawai'i Administrative Office	SRV Associations'	SRV Oregon	SRV San Francisco
PO Box 1364	website: www.srv.org	1922 SE 42nd Ave.,	Various Locations
Honoka'a, HI 96727	email: srvinfo@srv.org	Portland, OR 97215	Contact: srvinfo@srv.org
	Phone: 808-990-3354	Ph: 503-774-2410	or 808-990-3354

January, 2020

SRV San Francisco
1/11 Sun 9:30am Class: Tejabindu Upanisad
TBA,: call 808-990-3354

SRV Oregon (Call for meditation times)
1/15 Wed 7:00pm Bhagavad Gita, with Anurag
1/17 Fri 7:00pm Satsang, Swami Viveknanda's Birthday
1/18 Sat 9:30am Class: Akshi Upanisad
        6:00pm **Swami Vivekananda Puja**
1/19 Sun 9:30am Class: Akshi Upanisad
1/22 Wed 7:00pm Principles of the Upanisads, with Anurag
1/23 - 1/27 SRV Winter Retreat on the Oregon Coast

SRV Winter Retreat, January 23-27th, Oregon
Subject: Swami Vivekananda Vijnanagita II
Select Verses with Commentary and Contemplation
(arrive Thursday night 23rd, depart Monday 27th at noon)
For details on all retreats, see Retreat Pages

2020 SRV India Pilgrimage to Varanasi, City of Siva
With time in Kolkata & Chennai
Dates TBA
Study of Bhagavad Gita With Babaji in Varanasi

May, 2020

SRV San Francisco
5/10 Sun 9:30am Class: Tejabindu Upanisad (Mother's Day)
TBA,: call 808-990-3354

SRV Oregon (Call for meditation times)
5/13 Wed 7:00pm Bhagavad Gita, with Anurag
5/15 Fri 7:00pm Satsang with Babaji
5/16 Sat 9:30am Class: Akshi Upanisad
        6:00pm SRV Puja, Siva Puja
5/17 Sun 9:30am Class: Akshi Upanisad
5/20 Wed 7:00pm Principles of the Upanisads, with Anurag
5/21 - 5/25 Memorial Weekend Retreat, Windward Waters

Memorial Day Weekend Retreat, May 21-25th
Subject: Raja Yoga:
A Full Course on the Authentic 8 Limbs of Patanjali's Yoga
Location: Windwood Waters (Wind River Region, WA)
(arrive Thursday evening 21st, depart Monday 25th at noon)
For details, see Retreat Pages

Visit srv.org for all retreat details
Weekend Classes webcasted, 9:30 am to 12:30 pm, Pacific Time

July, 2020

2020 SRV Hawaii Retreat #1, Summer
July 3-7th, Swamiji's Mahasamadhi & Gurupurnima
Subject: True Freedom According to Indian Darshanas
(arrive Friday evening 3rd, depart Tuesday 7th at noon)

SRV San Francisco
8/6 Thu SRV SF Summer Retreat Begins at Foresthill, CA.

SRV American River Retreat over Janmashtami
August 6-10th, Foresthill, CA
Subject: My Guru's Teachings III
A Completion of the Study & Contemplation of
Swami Aseseshanandaji's Teachings and Divine Utterances
(arrive Thursday evening 6th, depart Monday 10th at noon)

SRV Oregon (Call for meditation times)
8/12 Wed 7:00pm Bhagavad Gita, with Anurag
8/15 Sat 9:30am Class: Akshi Upanisad
        6:00pm **Sri Krishna Puja** with Chanting
8/16 Sun 9:30am Class: Akshi Upanisad
8/19 Wed 7:00pm Vedanta 101 with Annapurna Sarada
8/21 Fri 6:00pm Open Seminar Satsang with Babaji
8/22 & 23 Weekend Seminar

SRV Weekend Seminar, August 22 & 23
Subject: Jnanamritam Chalisa – "Like The Sky" Stotram III
2 classes Sat., 2 classes Sun.
More Singing, Discourse, Commentary, & Contemplation
on these 40 verses from the Avadhuta Gita

October, 2020

SRV San Francisco
10/11 Sun 9:30am Class: TBA, call 808-990-3354

SRV Oregon (Call for meditation times)
10/14 Wed 7:00pm Bhagavad Gita, with Anurag
10/17 Sat 9:30am Class: Akshi Upanisad
        6:00pm **Sri Durga Devi Puja**
10/18 Sun 9:30am Class: Akshi Upanisad
10/21 Wed 7:00pm Principles of the Upanisads, with Anurag
10/22 - 10/26 SRV Fall Retreat, Mindful Heart Forest Retreat

SRV Fall Navaratri Retreat, October 22-26th
Annapurna Upanisad (1st of three parts)
Location: Mindful Heart Forest Retreat Corbett, OR
(arrive Thursday evening 22nd, depart Monday 26th at noon)

2020 SRV Hawaii Retreat #2, Winter
December 11-15, Around Holy Mother's Birthday
Subject: Sri Sarada Vijnanagita & Chanting 108 Names of Sarada

---

Announcing 2020 SRV India Pilgrimage to the Holy City of Siva
Date TBA   Inquire for Reservation

Destination: Varanasi, with time in Kolkata & Chennai (contact Babaji - babaji@hialoha.net)

SRV Vedanta Associations
Babaji's Teaching Schedule, 2020
SRV Hawai'i Retreat Center & Ashram

Hawaii Summer Retreat: Over Gurupurnima
Title: *Freedom According to Indian Darshanas*
Location: Paauilo, Big Island of Hawaii
July 3rd - 7th, 2020

Sunday Live Streaming Classes, 2:30 - 5:30pm
Hawai'i SRV Ashram   Directions: Call: 808-990-3354

- **Successful Mantra Practice**
  February 9th, 16th, & 23rd, 2020
- **The "Third Eye" — Kundalini's Sixth Chakra**
  March, 8th & 15th, 2020
- **Brahmapada: The Four Feet of Brahman**
  How Consciousness Disports Itself
  April 12th, 19th, & 26th, 2020
- **Sri Ram's Discourse of Divine Discontent**
  June 7th, 14th, 21st, 2020
- **Prana: The Missing Link**
  July 12th, 19th, & 26th, 2020
- **Points & Principles of Brahman**
  September 6th, 13th, 20th, & 27th, 2020
- **The Path, Neti Neti: The Tool, Viveka**
  Separating The Wheat From The Chaff
  November 8th, 15th, 22nd, & 29th, 2020
- **Vedanta, Theology, and Science**
  December 20th, & 27th, 2020

Hawaii Winter Retreat
Title: *Sri Sarada Vijnanagita:*
Holy Mother's Song of Wisdom
And Chanting of the 108 Names of Sarada
Location: Paauilo, Big Island of Hawaii
December 11th - 15th, 2020

Also, check www.srv.org for Hawaii retreats
or see our Retreats Pages in the back of this issue
Sign up for:
- SRV Magazine: Nectar of Non-Dual Truth
- Raja Yoga email study with Babaji
- SRV's Facebook page
- SRV's YouTube channel: Teaching videos

SRV Hawai'i Administrative Office:
PO Box 1364
Honoka'a, HI 96727
Ph: 808-990-3354

SRV Associations' website:
www.srv.org
email:
srvinfo@srv.org

See our SRV Facebook Page   facebook.com/srv.vedanta

SRV Vedanta Associations Website
www.srv.org
srvinfo@srv.org

Visit www.srv.org to find:
SRV's Livestream Channel
Webcast Time Zone Schedule

SRV's YouTube Channel Class Series
- Advaita of the Avatars
- Devotion of Nonseparation
- The Wisdom Particle
- The Non-Touch Yoga of Gaudapada
- Tibetan Buddhism & Advaita Vedanta
- Mother's Path of Nonduality
- Food, Prana, & Sadhana
- Brahman Reflected in the Universe
- Mind as the Kingdoms Of Heaven
- Destroying the Rust of Spiritual Life
- Advaita Vedanta's 6 Proofs of Truth
- Satsangs with Babaji
- Spiritual Interviews
- Music Videos
- Short Teachings

Explore our Website links to find:
- Sanskrit Chants to learn/practice
- Devotional Songs
- "In The Spirit" Audio Interviews

Teachings:
- SRV's Teachings for Youth/Children

Magazine:
- Order back issues of Nectar
- View our online archive of Nectar

Dharma Teachings & Sangha News
- Mundamala – SRV Sangha e-magazine
- SRV Sangha e-newsletter

SRV Associations — Retreats for 2020

SRV Oregon Coast Retreat
January 23rd - 27th, 2020, Nehalem, Oregon
Retreat Topic: *Swami Vivekananda Vijnanagita II*

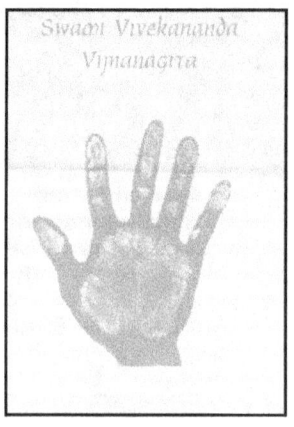

The import of Swami Vivekananda's visit to the West, and to America in particular, cannot be underestimated and should never be forgotten. Though surging like an underground river towards the surface, and carrying profound ramifications with it, the force of this great soul's presence on Western shores has already begun to produce candidates for enlightenment and jivamukti-hood among the few. How could it be otherwise, when he brought with him not only ancient India's noble Vedanta with its pure, advaitic expression, but also the divine presence of Sri Ramakrishna and Sri Sarada Devi within him? Now, it only remains for the awakened souls who recognize this spiritual phenomenon as the divine descent of the age, to adjust to the fresh start of a new religion amongst them, perform the necessary and called-for practices of purification, and claim their divine heritage.

SRV's winter retreat along the Oregon Coast will focus in on some of the main teachings of the Great Swami, all contemplated in the pristine coastal regions around Nehalem, Oregon, right across the street from the vast forested acres of Nehalem Bay State Park. Peace, quiet, and amazing ocean views will complement this lofty spiritual experience.

Location: Oregon Coast, Nehalem, Oregon
Arrival: Thursday, January 23rd, between 4 & 6pm
Departure: Monday, January 27th, by 12:00 noon
Tuition (all inclusive): $645; students $420   **Registration:** Begins now. Tuition is due by January 1st
Financial hardship? Call 808-990-3354   **Register by email:** srvinfo@srv.org or by phone 808-990-3354

SRV Spring Retreat Over Memorial Day Weekend
May 21st – 25th, 2020, at Windwood Waters.
Wind River region, Stevenson, Washington
Retreat Topic: *A Full Course on Patanjali's Raja Yoga*

The noble Eight-Limbed Yoga of Lord Patanjali has still to fully arrive in the West, and this is due, in part, to Europe and America's preoccupation with yoga of a physical kind only. In this retreat, the emphasis will begin with teachings on the abiding features of yama and niyama, such as nonviolence, study of scriptures, and deep devotion to God. The five crucial steps in between the first two limbs and the eighth — Raja's crowning glory of Samadhi — will also receive a detailed scrutiny so as to ensure a full understanding of this most comprehesive spiritual pathway.

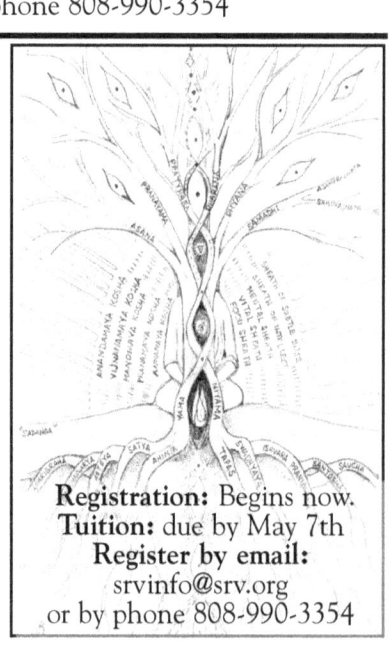

Location: Windwood Waters retreat site near Stevenson, WA
Arrival: Thursday, May 21st, by 9:00 pm
Departure: Monday, May 25th, noon
Tuition (all-inclusive): $690; Students: $425
Financial hardship? Call 808-990-3354

Registration: Begins now.
Tuition: due by May 7th
Register by email: srvinfo@srv.org
or by phone 808-990-3354

SRV American River Janmashtami Retreat, 2020

August 6th – 10th, 2020, Foresthill, CA
Subject: *My Guru's Teachings III: The conclusion of the series on Swami Aseshananda's unique look at spiritual life and practice in America.*

Part one and two of this series proved to be a *tour de force* concerning deep glimpses into both the history of America and how it has molded humanity's thinking process, and to what degree this type of thinking has influenced the modern day psyche of the Western individual. The swami's teachings focused in on traditional Vedanta and its Advaitic elements, no doubt, but were interspersed with clues and encouragements as to how to render human nature divine along the path of a tried and true method. His teachings on giving up violence, domination, and love of power were particularly potent, and thus he exhorted his American congregation to gain liberation, live consciously in a Self-realized State, and follow through on earth and in daily life with dedicated service to God in mankind.

Location: Private land in Foresthill, California, near the American River
Arrival: Thursday, August 6th, by 9pm,
Last day of retreat: Monday, August 10th (approximately noon, clean up follows)
Tuition (all inclusive): Adults: $570, students: $345   Daily rate, $160/$100, student
Registration: Begins now. Tuition is due by July 25th
Register by email: srvinfo@srv.org or by phone 808-990-3354
Financial hardship? Call 808-990-3354

SRV Fall Columbus Day Retreat, 2020

October 22nd – 26th, 2020, Location: Mindful Heart Forest Retreat
Subject: *The Seven Goddess Upanisads: <u>Annapurna Upanisad</u>, Pt.1*

The SRV Sangha and friends have studied the Devi Upanisad, Sita Upanisad, Saubaghya Lakshmi Upanisad, Savitri Upanisad, Yoga Kundalini Upanisad, and the Tripura Upanisad over 6 Autumn retreats. The 7th feather in our scriptural cap of Mother Upanisads will be part 1 of a deep inspection of the Annapurna Upanisad.

Location: Mindful Heart Forest Retreat, Corbett, Oregon
Arrival: Thursday, Oct 22nd
Departure: Monday, Oct 26th, 12:00 noon
Tuition: Adults: $450: Students: $225, Lodging/Meals, TBA
Registration: Begins now. Tuition by October 8th
Financial hardship? Call 808-990-3354 to discuss options
Register by email: srvinfo@srv.org or by phone 808-990-3354

SRV Summer Seminar in 2020, August 22nd & 23rd, Portland, Oregon, SRV Ashram

Subject: *Jnanamritam Chalisa III — "Like The Sky" Stotram*
Chanting, Discourse, Commentary, and Contemplation of these Forty Verses from the Avadhuta Gita

Schedule: Friday, August 21st: 6:00 PM – Seminar Satsang
Saturday, August 22nd: 6:00am – 5:00pm (meditation, breakfast, morning and afternoon classes, dinner)
Sunday, August 23rd: 6:00am – 5:00pm (meditation, breakfast, morning and afternoon classes)
Tuition (all-inclusive): $260; student, $130
Registration: Begins now. Tuition due by August 7th
Financial hardship? Call 808-990-3354 to discuss options
Register by email: srvinfo@srv.org or by phone 808-990-3354
Accommodations: This is a non-residential seminar

SRV Associations — Hawaii Retreat #1 for 2020

July 3rd - July 7th, 2020, On Vivekananda's Mahasamadhi (4th) & Gurupurnima (5th)
Retreat Topic: *Freedom/Mukti According to Indian Darshanas*

Moksha, Mukti, Kaivalya, Satta-Samanya — profound appellations such as these in India are in reference to and stand as testament to the eternal state of unbounded Liberation. Vedanta calls it Nirvikalpa Samadhi, Yoga calls it Asamprajnata, "seedless." Buddhism terms it Nirvana. In Japan, Zen refers to it as Satori. The luminaries say that It is not to be gained or attained, but beings longing after It duly remember It, and get free. What is this singular freedom like, and what does Its realization require of the sincere aspirant seeking perfection?

On Divine Mother's Mani Dvipa Jewel Island of Essence, affectionately known as the Big Island of Hawaii, and occurring auspiciously over the sacred periods of Swami Vivekananda's Mahasamadhi on July 4th and Gurupurnima on July 5th, retreatants will come face to face with the facets of true Freedom as seen and known by the holy hosts of India's rishis, sages, and seers throughout yugas. Their cogent instructions on salient practices will release the embodied soul from bondage — to matter, to form, to conventions, and to nature.

> "....the nondual scriptures point the way to the Supreme Moksha, that most elevated condition that is the very atmosphere of Divine Reality, all-abiding and all-pervading. The ordinary scriptures, as one can easily see by looking at the hosts of unillumined beings who refer to them as the highest authority, lead to bondage to the worlds of name and form, containing within them, as they do, an abundance of mundane worldly advice that insists upon attempting to satisfy one's desires in the world, amidst the objects of the world. Thus, spiritual wisdom, sought by the wise, and terrestrial knowledge, pursued by the worldly — these two ought to be examined for their respective merits and properties."   A Quintessential Yoga Vasishtha, Babaji Bob Kindler

Location: SRV Retreat Center on the Hamakua Coast, Big Island of Hawaii
Arrival: Friday, July 3rd, by 6pm
Departure: Tuesday, July 7th, at 12:00 noon
Tuition, Meals, & Lodging: Shared rooms, $515/person; Private room, $565; Tenting, $415-465/person
Registration: Begins now. Tuition is due by June 9th
Register by email: srvinfo@srv.org or by phone 808-990-3354
Financial hardship? Contact us to learn about options.

Student Rates: Shared — $360
Platform — $310
Tent — $260 (Same rates the Retreat #2)

SRV Associations — Hawaii Retreat #2 for 2020

December 11th - 15th, 2020, Big Island of Hawaii
Retreat Topic: Sri Sarada Vijnanagita (over Holy Mother's Birthday)
"I bless you upon this holy day that you might attain liberation in this life." Sri Sarada Vijnanagita

Dove-tailing an indepth study and recitation of the precious book, *Sri Sarada Vijnanagita*, with the group chanting of the 108 Names of Sarada, the winter retreat on the Big Island of Hawaii will transmit vast and deep spiritual power to all who choose to attend upon it. It will be attended with ocean vistas, comfortable quarters, sattvic vegetarian food, and abundant time for classes, private study, and meditation — all in a location that is fully dedicated to sincere pursuit of the spiritual path. Peace of mind is here, as well as all that is necessary to prepare the aspiring soul for rapt refuge and full abidance within the ecstatic transcendent atmosphere of the Great Self.

"Tvam Me Brahma Sanatani Ma, Sarada Ishvari Subhage Ma" — with this profound and endearing opening verse, the "108 Names of Sarada" begin to relate to the captivated and divinely intoxicated chanter the ancient and mostly forgotten secrets of Eastern spirituality, and usher him/her into an interior realm that is ripe with divine Love and rife with living Intelligence.

Location: Hamakua, Big Island of Hawaii   **Arrival:** Friday, December 11th, by 6pm
Departure: Tuesday, December 15th, at 12:00 noon
Tuition, Meals, & Lodging: Shared rooms, $515/person; Private room, $565; Tenting, $415-465/person
Registration: Begins now. Tuition is due by November 27th
Register by email: srvinfo@srv.org or by phone 808-990-3354 **Financial hardship?** Contact us to learn options.

Donation/Order Form
Suggested donation $15 per issue

Nectar #36 is available for free if you write, email, or call for a copy by January 15, 2021.
Your generous donations make Nectar available to others.
Those who donate $15 or more for the next issue will be added our subscribers list.

☐ Please send me/my friend a free copy of the next issue of Nectar.
☐ Send me ____ copies to give to friends, Spiritual Centers, or a business of my choice. (fill out back of form)
☐ I want to make sure there are future issues of Nectar ($200 and up)

Nectar needs sustaining donors! ($500 and up) Your gift is tax-deductible.

Please fill out the back side of this form and mail it with your check to:
SRV Associations, PO Box 1364, Honokaa, HI 96727
MasterCard or Visa accepted • Make checks payable to: SRV Associations
808-990-3354 • srvinfo@srv.org • www.srv.org

#35

Donation/Order Form
Suggested donation $15 per issue

Nectar #36 is available for free if you write, email, or call for a copy by January 15, 2021.
Your generous donations make Nectar available to others.
Those who donate $15 or more for the next issue will be added our subscribers list.

☐ Please send me/my friend a free copy of the next issue of Nectar.
☐ Send me ____ copies to give to friends, Spiritual Centers, or a business of my choice. (fill out back of form)
☐ I want to make sure there are future issues of Nectar ($200 and up)

Nectar needs sustaining donors! ($500 and up) Your gift is tax-deductible.

Please fill out the back side of this form and mail it with your check to:
SRV Associations, PO Box 1364, Honokaa, HI 96727
MasterCard or Visa accepted • Make checks payable to: SRV Associations
808-990-3354 • srvinfo@srv.org • www.srv.org

#35

Donation/Order Form
Suggested donation $15 per issue

Nectar #36 is available for free if you write, email, or call for a copy by January 15, 2021.
Your generous donations make Nectar available to others.
Those who donate $15 or more for the next issue will be added our subscribers list.

☐ Please send me/my friend a free copy of the next issue of Nectar.
☐ Send me ____ copies to give to friends, Spiritual Centers, or a business of my choice. (fill out back of form)
☐ I want to make sure there are future issues of Nectar ($200 and up)

Nectar needs sustaining donors! ($500 and up) Your gift is tax-deductible.

Please fill out the back side of this form and mail it with your check to:
SRV Associations, PO Box 1364, Honokaa, HI 96727
MasterCard or Visa accepted • Make checks payable to: SRV Associations
808-990-3354 • srvinfo@srv.org • www.srv.org

#35

Your Information:

Name: _____

Address: _____

City, State, Zip: _____

Email: _____

Additional Address: (please use a sheet of paper for more addresses)

Name: _____

Address: _____

City, State, Zip: _____

Email: _____

Do you wish to pay by Mastercard or Visa?

Card No.: _____ **Amount:** _____

Exp. date: _____ **Phone no.:** _____

Signature: _____

Questions? call SRV Associations: 808-990-3354

Your Information:

Name: _____

Address: _____

City, State, Zip: _____

Email: _____

Additional Address: (please use a sheet of paper for more addresses)

Name: _____

Address: _____

City, State, Zip: _____

Email: _____

Do you wish to pay by Mastercard or Visa?

Card No.: _____ **Amount:** _____

Exp. date: _____ **Phone no.:** _____

Signature: _____

Questions? call SRV Associations: 808-990-3354

Your Information:

Name: _____

Address: _____

City, State, Zip: _____

Email: _____

Additional Address: (please use a sheet of paper for more addresses)

Name: _____

Address: _____

City, State, Zip: _____

Email: _____

Do you wish to pay by Mastercard or Visa?

Card No.: _____ **Amount:** _____

Exp. date: _____ **Phone no.:** _____

Signature: _____

Questions? call SRV Associations: 808-990-3354

www.ingramcontent.com/pod-product-compliance
Lightning Source LLC
Chambersburg PA
CBHW080024110526
44587CB00021BA/3840